T0267368

MANOJ
BAJPAYEE

MANOJ BAJPAYEE

The DEFINITIVE BIOGRAPHY

PIYUSH PANDEY

EBURY
PRESS

An imprint of Penguin Random House

EBURY PRESS

USA | Canada | UK | Ireland | Australia
New Zealand | India | South Africa | China | Singapore

Ebury Press is part of the Penguin Random House group of companies
whose addresses can be found at global.penguinrandomhouse.com

Published by Penguin Random House India Pvt. Ltd
4th Floor, Capital Tower 1, MG Road,
Gurugram 122 002, Haryana, India

Penguin
Random House
India

First published in Ebury Press by Penguin Random House India 2024

Copyright © Piyush Pandey and Rohit Vats 2024

Translated by Rohit Vats

All rights reserved

10 9 8 7 6 5 4 3 2 1

ISBN 9780143466925

Typeset in Adobe Garamond Pro by MAP Systems, Bengaluru, India
Printed at Thomson Press India Ltd, New Delhi

www.penguin.co.in

For my father, Prakash Mohan Pandey,
with whom I went to watch my first-ever film in a theatre—
Dostana,
and I forced him to leave the film just after the beginning
as Mr Amitabh Bachchan opened fire on screen

Contents

A Note from Manoj Bajpayee

Piyush Pandey has penned my biography. I hope readers find it interesting and unique. Frankly, I don't think there is anything extraordinary about my life, yet I am hopeful they will find this biography interesting. I can't say for sure if it will be inspirational because my life doesn't resemble that of a big politician or philosopher from whom you can learn something or take inspiration. But I am hopeful the journey Piyush is taking you on with his writing will thrill you, keeping you glued to the book till its last page.

My good wishes to Piyush.

Manoj Bajpayee

Preface

What was the need for a book on Manoj Bajpayee? you might ask.

I was stunned after watching *Satya* at Agra's Shah Talkies in July/August 1998. Intensely mesmerized by Bhiku Mhatre (played by Manoj), I couldn't figure out where to start writing about the actor. My journalism career hadn't started, and it wasn't the era of social media either. However, I requested everyone at home to watch *Satya* at the earliest. The way Manoj portrayed the character was not only fascinating but also mysterious.

Even if he hadn't done any other film after *Satya*, Manoj would have his name 'registered' in the history of Hindi films. Thankfully, he has films such as *Shool* (1999), *Kaun* (1999), *Pinjar* (2003), *Gangs of Wasseypur* (2012), *Aligarh* (2015), *Gali Guleiyan* (2017) and *Bhonsle* (2018) to his credit—projects that can have an entire chapter dedicated to him in the history of Hindi films.

More than talking about his acting prowess, the reason why this book has been written is to chronicle Manoj's struggles as an actor, which is no less than a film in itself. There are so many twists and turns in his journey—from Bettiah to Bollywood—that you find yourself on his side in the battle against fate.

I have known Manoj for fifteen years—since the time senior journalist Punya Prasun Bajpai requested him to write on my blogging platform.

I worked for a year as an editorial consultant with Bihar and Jharkhand's popular newspaper *Prabhat Khabar*. It was the time when I started the ace actor's column on the revered editorial page. While learning about Manoj's thought process and struggle, I realized that his life and career deserved a book. Being in close proximity to him prompted me to attempt a biography. This wouldn't have been possible without his cooperation, of course.

With this biography, I also intend to bring the real Manoj Bajpayee in front of everyone. The Internet is full of misleading information about him. For example, the story about his first marriage to a Bihar girl whom he allegedly left after becoming successful. Or, how he tried to die by suicide after failing the National School of Drama (NSD) entrance. It is an attempt to chaff the misinformation from the reality. Moreover, I also wanted to look at his journey through the eyes of his contemporaries.

Since I too, like Manoj, have grown up in a village, I could relate to his struggles and triumphs—his mammoth dream of making it big in Mumbai despite hailing from a village in Bihar. Because of dilapidated roads, a poor transport system and an extreme crime rate, moving from Bihar to Delhi in the 1980s was quite tough, leave aside moving to Mumbai. I have spent several years in a small township of Uttar Pradesh called Auraiya. After college, I applied for a course in direction at the Film and Television Institute of India (FTII), Pune, but there wasn't anyone in Agra to guide me. The English language was another hurdle. These are some of the challenges that we both share, given our backgrounds. So, I wanted to understand how Manoj went beyond the usual limits. The curiosity to find similarities forced me to pen down everything.

His inspirational journey has value beyond our imagination. Many such dreams have been documented in this book.

However, I will let the reader be the ultimate judge of the book, but I did thoroughly enjoy the process of compiling and writing it. Many film industry stalwarts became a part of my inner circle during the process.

Through this book, I hope to bring to the fore unheard-of tales from Manoj's life—stories that only close friends and family have been privy to. Say, for example, what exactly was the bone of contention between Manoj and Ram Gopal Varma, or Manoj and Anurag Kashyap?

Apart from highlighting interesting anecdotes, this biography will also put a stop to many rumours regarding his life.

I have also written in the hope of making the readers objective spectators of Manoj's layered journey at close quarters.

It's the first biography of Manoj Bajpayee, at least in the known realms of publication. I am happy that I have written it, and now it's in your hands. Sincere efforts have been made to make it error-free. I do not intend to hurt anyone in any manner.

In anticipation of your kindness and feedback.

Yours sincerely,
Piyush Pandey
Email: pandeypiyush07@gmail.com
Twitter: @pandeypiyush

Chapter 1

Sons of Champaran

'Babuji [my father] had heard of the Film and Television Institute of India (FTII) in Pune, and that prompted him to go there. Incidentally, auditions were happening on that day. He confided in us that he too participated. Interestingly, Manoj Kumar and Dharmendra were also there.'

The name Champaran owes its origin to 'Champa-aranya', literally meaning a land full of magnolias (champa flowers). A prominent spot during India's independence struggle, Champaran is deeply rooted in mystical mythologies. It is believed that Sita took shelter here during her exile and gave birth to the twins Luv and Kush. Here, you will also find monuments related to the Buddha. Legend has it that the Buddha crossed Champaran while moving to Kushinagar from Vaishali.

Through the Mughal era, and further till Mahatma Gandhi's first satyagraha, Champaran has always found a place in people's hearts. Mohandas transformed into the 'Mahatma' only after winning the battle against the British Raj in favour of the indigo farmers on this very land.

In 1972, East and West Champaran were created, with headquarters at Motihari and Bettiah, respectively, for administrative convenience, but the people and culture remained the same.

Belwa, a small village located in West Champaran, takes pride in being the birthplace of Manoj Bajpayee.

Shatrughan Sinha achieved much for Bihari actors in the film industry, and Manoj Bajpayee carried forward this legacy in style. There is a unique sense of inner strength around Manoj that usually comes with years of struggle and from not bending under pressure. The same stubbornness that got him out of many people's good books, so to say, is his identity today. However, his resolve to take up challenges head-on can be traced back to his family. His great-grandfather, Mahaveer Prasad Bajpayee, migrated from UP's Raebareli. The exact date couldn't be ascertained, but the move from Pasankher village to Bihar changed several things for the family's future. The oppressed villagers of that area in UP were getting together against the cruel Oudh Rent Act of 1886. This act empowered the zamindars and talukdars to evict and atrociously charge the farmers of twelve districts of the estate. Just like a film, it formed the perfect backdrop for a rebellion.

Sample this description, published in an essay: 'January 5, 1921, nearly three thousand farmers gheraoed the bungalow of Chandniha Estate's "tallukdar" Tribhuwanbahadur Singh. He informed the Deputy Commissioner AG Sheriff about the possibilities of loots and riots. Sheriff acted fast and reached the spot to get farmer leaders—Baba Janakidas, Pandit Amol Sharma and Chandrapal Singh—arrested. The leaders were presented in front of the magistrate and awarded imprisonment of one year. They were transferred overnight to the Lucknow Jail [translated from Hindi].'[1]

Meanwhile, a rumour was doing the rounds that the police had killed the arrested farmers on the cue of a woman close to Tribhuwanbahadur Singh. A group of men wanted to reach Raebareli and uncover the truth, but a heavy deployment of police on the other side of the Sai River stopped them from crossing it. Meanwhile, a face-off was brewing on the riverbanks. Another talukdar and local Member of the Legislative Council Sardar Veerpal Singh's mansion was nearby, and he feared that it might be attacked. He started firing bullets in the air after hearing loud slogans; the local police too joined in. Hundreds of farmers died. Legendary journalist Ganesh Shankar Vidyarthi called it 'one more Jallianwala' in *Pratap*.

Mahaveer Prasad Bajpayee probably reached Bihar around this time. Manoj's grandfather, Laxman Prasad Bajpayee, was the youngest among Mahaveer Prasad's three children. The two older brothers were into farming, and they really loved their younger brother Laxman. Unlike themselves, they wanted Laxman to study. As a result, Laxman was admitted to the local school. Thankfully, he turned out to be studious and passed the matriculation exam, which was a big achievement back then. Laxman wanted to go for higher studies, but Gandhi's call for satyagraha inspired him to discontinue his studies and join the movement.

Manoj Bajpayee's father, the late Radhakant Bajpayee, reminisced about those early years in a candid conversation with me: 'Babuji [Laxman Prasad Bajpayee] left his studies and was idle for a while. The satyagraha movement too had come to an end by then. Around that time, a factory was being set up in Narkatiaganj, whose manager was Ghanshyam Das Ramani. He came to know about this guy who was not only 'matric pass' but could also speak English. He offered Babuji a job. Babuji was tasked with promoting sugar cane cultivation in the vicinity. Ghanshyam Das really liked Babuji for his dedication. The Bajpayee family owned a sizeable portion of land, but there was hardly anyone who understood the nitty-gritties of farming. Babuji also had a job at the sugar cane *dharam kanta*[2]. He was also the one who distributed money among the farmers for better sugar cane provisions. This gave him a standing among the locals, but the brothers didn't approve of the nature of Laxman's job, and ultimately, he had to settle for full-time farming.'

Laxman had three sons: Kamalakant, Radhakant and Avdhesh Prasad. Kamalakant, a double MA, pursued politics. 'There were two lobbies in the Bihar Congress at that time: one led by Bibhuti Narayan Mishra and the other by Anugrah Narayan Singh,' says Manoj Bajpayee's brother Saroj. 'Despite being a Brahmin, Kamalakant [his uncle] supported the second fraction. He got furious with the party high command when he was not given the ticket from the Shikarpur assembly seat. He started campaigning in favour of Ramnagar's king, Maharaj Bibhuti Narayan Singh. The Congress expelled Kamalakant for six years for anti-party activities.'

The Bajpayees were living in Jadia village, which is close to the Harbora River, but they wanted to leave the place due to regular floods. The clan pressurized Kamalakant to buy Bibhuti Narayan Singh's Belwa mansion. Finally, on the recommendation of Narayan's wife, it was sold to the Bajpayee family for Rs 50,000 in 1957.

The *kothi* (bungalow) had its own history. Rajendra Prasad's book titled *Champaran Mein Mahatma Gandhi,* set in Champaran, has a reference to the seventy kothis that served as the offices of indigo plantation in 1917.[3] Every kothi was allotted a fixed area for supervision, with an English manager called *nilha* who was in charge. One of the oldest of these allotted areas belonged to Colonel Hikki in Bara. Every *raiyat* (farmer) was required to set aside 15 per cent of their land for indigo plantation. Despite it being a cash crop, the raiyats were not allowed to sell indigo to anybody other than the landowners, that too at a meagre price. Anyway, indigo was believed to destroy the land's productivity, but who would listen to them?

A.C. Emman was one particular nilha known for his conniving tactics. One incident is mentioned in *Champaran Mein Mahatma Gandhi*: 'On one night, around 10, a villager from Parsauni village had come to meet Gandhiji. He told Gandhiji about the atrocities he had to put up with due to his refusal of bowing down to Emman's unfair ways. He was also apprehensive about his property being looted on Emman's orders. This English manager was also responsible for pushing another farmer, Rajkumar Shukla, to meet Gandhiji. Eventually, they would start a movement together against the English management system.'[4]

Mahatma Gandhi once arrived at the Belwa kothi to meet Emman and stayed at the house of another villager called Sant Raut. This establishes Gandhi's association with the place. In a way, Gandhi was an integral part of the local folklore and, thus by association, Manoj's childhood. After all, this is the place where the ace actor grew up.

Gandhi also set up a school at the nearby Bhitiharwa Ashram, where he started his Champaran Satyagraha. Since nobody was willing to donate land for this ashram fearing the wrath of the British, a local saint named Ramnarayan Das gave up his land for the purpose. However, nothing stopped Emman from getting the ashram torched down. Gandhi managed to escape though. You will still find many artefacts related to Gandhi at this ashram.

It is hard to assess how much influence Gandhi's association with Champaran has on Manoj, but knowing such a heritage is an amazing feeling in itself.

Hobbies and legacies

Let me take you back to Manoj's father, Radhakant Bajpayee's, backstory and how his love for films induced a magical spark in young Manoj's subconscious. Radhakant studied BSc, which was a big deal in those days, from Muzaffarpur's Langat Singh College—an institution that saw contributions from the likes of Rajendra Prasad and Acharya J.B. Kripalani, apart from the famous social activist Langat Singh. Till date, the college hasn't lost its prominence and continues to produce leaders in various fields.

During college, Radhakant and his friends became film fanatics and watched the 'first day, first show' of every major release.

Muzaffarpur was then known for its many cinema halls— Shyam, Prabhat, Jawahar and Chitra, to name a few. He recalled his friend Hiranandan Rai, an English teacher at the Maharani Janki Kuwar College. With a sheepish smile, he admitted that he was a big fan of the legendary Dilip Kumar, who would go on to praise his son, Manoj, as an actor.

Manoj Bajpayee describes his meeting with one of India's biggest movie stars, Dilip Kumar, in a 2011 blog.[5] It was at the wedding of his friend, Dr Shrilata Suresh Trasi's daughter. He remembers fondly how Dilip Saab, the 'living legend', agreed to meet him despite his frail health at that time, thanks to Saira Banu, Dilip Saab's wife. 'The way he greeted me, it felt like the world's biggest gift,' recalls an emotional Manoj.

In April 2003, there was a *Times of India* report of Dilip Kumar and Manoj Bajpayee working in a film together, to be supposedly directed by Tinnu Anand, but it never materialized.[6] Radhakant Bajpayee regretted this to his last day. Alas, Manoj couldn't share screen space with any of his father's favourites. 'I used to read *Filmfare* and watch many films. I liked Motilal and Dev Anand, apart from Dilip Kumar. Motilal and Dilip Kumar were actors, but Dev Anand was a *hero*. Come to think of it, my son [Manoj] also received more fame as an *actor* than a *hero* in his career.'

The story of Radhakant Bajpayee's obsession with films has many dimensions. Manoj's elder sister Kamini Shukla recalls: 'While cleaning our house during the Chhath festival, we found a prospectus of the Pune Film Institute in Father's belongings. Manoj also saw it. Then our father revealed how his college's botany department had taken them on a trip to Pune. Because he had heard of the institute, he went to the campus. Auditions were taking place at that time. He too auditioned for an acting course. The interesting thing is the presence of Manoj Kumar and Dharmendra in the campus during the same time.'

Everybody knows about Manoj Kumar and Dharmendra's friendship. Rajiv M. Vijayakar's biography on Dharmendra mentions how he had to wait two years for a break despite being a Filmfare Talent Hunt discovery.[7] Kamini adds, 'Babuji might have been interested in acting, but he had no preparation. He just acted upon chance.'

How different would it have been for Manoj if his father was selected in the FTII acting course!

Radhakant, during his college days, also worked as a part-time 'Film Babu' in his spare time. He was responsible for taking a film's reel box to theatres from distributors. He would bring the reel box from Patna to Muzaffarpur.

The seeds of rebellion

Radhakant wanted to be a doctor after completing his BSc but missed the medical college merit list with half a percentage. 'My brother was a famous politician, yet I couldn't get admission. I left studies as I came to realize that things don't always turn out as planned,' he laments. 'I got married in the second year of college. My brother-in-law was studying engineering in Jamshedpur at that time. He sent me the application form of a medical college. I could have gotten admission there, but I had to pay Rs 5000 as donation. Tuition fee of two years and hostel fee were included in this. I asked Babuji about this, but he plainly refused. This only convinced me further to discontinue my studies.'

Radhakant could have asked his father-in-law, who was a police officer, for money, but he decided against it. Later, he got an earful from his father-in-law for not having asked.

Maybe it was his destiny to become a farmer or to be known as his 'son's father', but it was one regret that remained with Radhakant till his last days. He passed away in October 2021.

Another leaf from Radhakant Bajpayee's life is an incident about a tractor that his cousin had received from their in-laws' house, which nobody knew how to drive. Somebody asked Radhakant if he could start the machine of the 'beast'.

While narrating the incident, Radhakant told me, 'I was rebellious at that time. I said yes despite not knowing how to drive the tractor. So, I just walked around it a few times and then asked some people to push it. Eventually, the ignition started and that is how I learnt to drive the tractor. I also learnt how to plough the field with a tractor.'

Before Manoj's birth, Radhakant had once gone to Delhi to buy a Jeep for an acquaintance. After buying it for Rs 30,000 and getting it registered in Mayapuri, he drove it back to Belwa. The story of him getting his driving licence is also interesting. 'I went to the superintendent's office for a trial in Bettiah. The deputy superintendent of police [DSP] was there. He asked me for my learner's licence, and I showed it to him. Later, he came to the Jeep and asked me to take him to MJK College. While returning, he asked me to stop on the Kachahari Road. He then instructed me to take the Jeep towards a truck on the other side of the road. I refused, despite knowing he was the DSP. I was very categorical about not driving on the wrong side of the road. He questioned my "attitude", but I explained how my driving on the wrong side could cause a traffic jam and then the DSP would have himself denied licence. He started laughing and upon reaching his office gave orders to change my learner's licence into a permanent one!'

Radhakant was enterprising and kept trying his luck in various fields. He remained the village sarpanch for years. This might be an indication of how Manoj also saw life, and how he was not ready to give up in the face of adversities.

Like his father, Manoj too is frank and honest, and this has not gone down well with some of his relatives. If the rebel bone in Manoj can be traced back to his father, his mother, Geeta Devi, is the one who instilled a sense of discipline in him. His mother, who also passed away in December 2022, told me, 'Manoj has always seen me as a disciplined person, and he has inherited that trait from me. He promised to attend college every day upon getting admission. When he decides to do something, he puts his heart and soul into it.'

Manoj, in some of his interviews, called his father and mother perfect 'filmchi' (avid film watchers). When I went to meet Manoj's parents at his sister's house in Ghaziabad, his mother was watching a film—not Hindi, but Bhojpuri. Dinesh Lal Yadav Nirhaua was the lead actor. Her simplicity was simply unbelievable. She seemed totally unaware of her son's accomplishments and how Manoj has become an institution in himself.

Chapter 2

Belwa Days

'I am confident even if my name was "donkey", people would have said that the donkey has done a remarkable job in Satya, *deserved the National Award for* Pinjar *and has done a commendable job in a comic role in* Money Hai Toh Honey Hai. *What's in a name?'*

Manoj Bajpayee was born in Bettiah's Maharani Janki Kunwar Hospital. The historic hospital was built in 1892 by the then king of Bettiah Estate, Raja Sir Harendra Kishore Singh Bahadur. Built at a cost of Rs 40,897, it was then called Lady Dufferin Hospital. The hospital had AIIMS-like management under the leadership of T.K. Sundaram. It was converted into a government medical college in 2007.

Confusion about birth year

Manoj's parents had lost a newborn earlier, so his well-being was a concern for them. Manoj's official birthdate is 23 April 1969. The late Geeta Devi told me, 'Manoj was born around 3 p.m. We lived in the village but used to regularly come to the city a month prior to delivery.'

Manoj's siblings—Kamini, Saroj, Poonam, Sujit and Garima—were also born in the same hospital and so were some of his cousins. The hospital must have given us some kind of a deal, is still a family joke!

Manoj, in some of his interviews, has said that he came to Delhi in 1983, when he was seventeen years of age. He spoke in a BBC interview that he 'watched the colour television for the first time after coming to Delhi in 1983 [translated from Hindi]'.[8]

That year, he wouldn't have been more than fourteen years old as per his official birthdate. It is unusual for a kid of that age to live alone in Delhi. Also, if he did come to Delhi after clearing his higher secondary, he would have been more than sixteen or seventeen years of age. 'I can't remember the year, but the date was definitely 23 April,' said his mother.

Manoj, in the piece titled 'Belwa Diary' in the *Outlook* magazine, remembers his school days: 'My early education happened at a small school near my village. Till class II, I used to sit on a jute sack laid on the bare ground in the class. My teacher was my resident master at home as well. My father had provided him accommodation so my classes could continue beyond regular school timings. Despite the proximity of family, it was not uncommon to get a whacking from mastersaab!'[9]

Gyandev Tripathi, one of Manoj's childhood friends, says, 'There was a school beside English officer A.C. Emman's office. It's a pucca building now under the "Education for All" movement by the government.'

The confusion about the birth year might have started when Manoj moved to a school in Bettiah. During those times, many parents deliberately reduced their wards' birth year in anticipation of longer functioning years, if they managed to land a government job later. It was an accepted norm to reduce the age in school documents.

In contrast, Manoj's *janmpatri* (horoscope) had the correct birth time and location. In fact, the astrologer had predicted his unique life on the basis of his janampatri. Manoj's father told me, 'Bettiah's astrologer Panchanand Mishra was very categorical in his prediction that the boy is going to receive big fame. He was either going to be a politician or an actor.' That old janmpatri is not with the family now. Apparently, it's with Manoj!

Manoj hasn't shown any interest in politics so far. In fact, in a recent interaction with journalist Sudhir Chaudhary on Aaj Tak's *Seedhi Baat*, he confessed to being not inclined towards politics. When asked, 'What if Modiji asks you to contest elections?', he said, 'I will ask for forgiveness with folded hands.'[10] Manoj has another story as to why he stays away from politics. 'Years ago, I watched a Hungarian film titled *Mephisto* at Shakuntalam. The film showcases the rise and fall of a person close to the government. The depiction remained in my heart. That's why I keep a distance from politics.'

'We had a meeting with Nitish Kumar in 2010 where he subtly hinted to Manoj to join his party,' says Manoj's journalist-friend Anuranjan Jha.

I recall asking Manoj in 2009 if he would like to contest elections if he was offered a ticket. He had a clear-cut 'no' as answer.

Story behind the name

Manoj's father Radhakant Bajpayee, who was a Manoj Kumar fan, told me that he had named his son after the actor. It's a different matter that Manoj didn't like his name for a long time. 'It's a very common name in Bihar. Manoj Tyrewala, Manoj Bhujiawala, Manoj Meatwala, and what not! You'll find so many similar names in Bihar. I had thought of changing my name. In fact, I wanted to be called Samar. In my theatre days, I was told that changing one's name is a legal process, and I would have to get an affidavit made and then place an ad in a newspaper. This would have taken some money, so I thought of getting it done after earning a little. When I earned some money after *Bandit Queen*, I thought of finally doing it, but my brother said people would find Manoj Bajpayee in your first film and some other name in the consequent projects. So, I dropped the idea eventually.'

As the Bard said: what's in a name?

'I have expressed pride to Manoj Kumar-ji so many times about me being named after him. When I was thinking of a name change, my father stopped me from doing so. After all he had named me with so much love and affection!'

Ironically, Manoj Kumar himself had a name change. His birth name was Harikrishan Giri Goswami. Not many know that Harikishan was a huge fan of Dilip Kumar. He decided to name himself after Dilip Kumar's on-screen character Manoj Kumar after watching the film *Shabnam*.

Manoj Bajpayee has written in a long blog post titled 'Name, Computer and I': 'The process of selecting a name for the kid begins long before his arrival. Chinku, Pinku, Aamir, Raj or Manoj! I was never concerned about it because it seemed 99 thousand names out of a lakh is Manoj. And then what's in a name! So, when my friend Prasoon inspired me to start a blog, I was worried more about the name than the theme!'[11]

'In fact, when another friend who helped me set up the blog (yours truly) told me the name of the blog is "Manoj Bajpai", I was kind of sad, because this is not the correct spelling of my name. The official spelling is Manoj Bajpayee, which the media and the film people have never used. When I tried to talk about it, I was accused of using numerology. Though I have no problems with any sorts of maths, science, or any other belief.'

'Suppose you call an owl "Manoj", the people would have said that Manoj remains awake at night. Wouldn't have made any difference! Anyway, my spelling was finally changed, nothing changed but I was satisfied.'

The village within

Manoj is now Belwa's biggest identity. The late Geeta Devi told me, 'There are two Belwas, but our Belwa is known for Manoj.'

Belwa is an integral part of Manoj. 'Belwa is the most beautiful village in this universe. Let me give you a visual. You wake up in the morning and see the Himalayan range. During winters,

you see the sunrays reflecting from the glaciers. The winters are
terribly cold, and the summers are agonisingly hot. There is a
dense forest, which is now modified into a tiger reserve, some
four kilometres away. Recently, I visited, and the ranger told me
that there are around thirty-two tigers in the reserve. You couldn't
be sure though because the Indo-Nepal border is very porous
and tigers from both the regions keep mingling. So, it's hard to
ascertain whether it's thirty-two or 132. The land is so fertile that
all you need to do is spread seeds and the rest is taken care of by
nature. Our house has a river on one side and a canal on the other.
The river is called "Hadbadua" as it is a hilly river, which is always
in a hurry.'

During his childhood days, Manoj was quite shy. His mother
told me, 'He was shy and introverted, but that changed after he
cleared his intermediate exam. As a child, Manoj had stomach-
related issues, so he looked a bit weak and frail.'

'I was more mischievous. He [Manoj] used to take me along
in case of any fights,' confesses Manoj's younger brother Saroj,
who was of a sturdier build.

However, being shy wasn't any hindrance when it came to
having fun with close friends. Playing by the canal was a favourite
hobby for the children of the household. Later, Manoj took up
hunting. 'We used to go hunting in the nearby forests as it wasn't
banned in those days,' says Manoj's friend Rajkumar Singh. 'We
did the same during the release of *Satya* as well. Some friends from
Mumbai had also come, but the vehicle broke down in the jungle
and that scared all of us.'

Manoj is a foodie too, his all-time favourite being daal-chawal
and aalo-parwal.

Belwa was also the place where he was introduced to a
deep essence of religion. His grandfather regaled the children
with mythological stories and that sowed the seeds for a sense
of spirituality and religion in young Manoj's mind. There was
another incident that added a philosophical touch to his thought

process. His aunt died when he was eight. This was the first death he had seen, and it shook him from within. He hadn't thought of his parents' death until that day. That incident started an inward journey, so to say. Something would always be going on in his head, even though he looked peaceful from within. Such a thought process about life and death continues.

The family might be well-to-do farmers, but they too had their fair share of struggles. 'Ours was a joint family, with around 100 bighas of land. We had a share of twenty-five bighas. We didn't have cash but enough grain to get through the year,' recalled Manoj's mother. Plus, Manoj had five siblings whose education had to be paid for. However, he was happy while he lived in the village.

'It was an incredible childhood. We used to play hide-and-seek among rice sacks. We bathed in the canal. Now, when I go to the swimming pool with my daughter, she says, "You swim like a crazy person". Those who swim in rivers and canals, throw more punches than required,' says Manoj in an interview with Neelesh Misra.[12]

Kamini, recalling Manoj's naughtiness, says, 'Manoj and I would get into constant fights. He used to poke me. As we had no ceiling fans then, I used to clean up the floor and sleep on it during summers. Manoj and Saroj would snatch my pillow and bedsheet to annoy me. If I scolded them, they would threaten me with false complaints to our mother.'

It was in this village that Manoj heard his recorded voice for the first time. His father had bought a Panasonic tape recorder on his trip to Birgunj, a city in Nepal, and Manoj recorded his voice on it.

Chapter 3

Bettiah Days

'Acting was always there inside my heart and I wanted to do nothing else, but it wasn't seen as a respectable profession, so I kept the desire buried.'

'We have reached Bettiah around 4 p.m. It was an incredible experience. Every station on the way was filled with people, and the train had to stop for more than the required time. I had to greet people by coming to the gate at each juncture, but Bettiah took it a notch further. The train had to be stopped before [it reached] the platform because more than ten thousand people were in and around the tracks. When I came out, people wanted to fetch the cart instead of the horses. I tried to stop the crowd from doing so, but everything went in vain. They were cheering and showering flowers. All this is indicating towards something good. Maybe the almighty has some plans!'

This is the description of Gandhi's arrival in Bettiah on 22 April 1917, in his diary, as quoted by journalist Arvind Mohan in his book *Mr. MK Gandhi Ki Champaran Diary*.[13]

Gandhi wasn't wrong as this historic trip gave him the resolve to chase away the British Empire.

Even if one tries, it's hard to find a connection between the Mahatma and Manoj Bajpayee except for the fact that they both have M as the first letter of their names. However, one date can be of interest to the reader. Gandhi met farmer leader Raj Kumar Shukla on 23 April 1917 and blew the bugle of revolution— 23 April is Manoj's birth date as well.

Bettiah days

Manoj didn't know what to expect from life when he shifted to Bettiah. In fact, those were dark days. He was admitted in the third standard at a missionary school, and he lived in a dark and dirty lodge run by a staff teacher. He was bullied by his seniors, making those days a bad memory. He wanted to remain in the school campus as it kept the trauma of being in the lodge at bay.

He changed three schools in Bettiah: St Stanislaus (also known as Mission School), where he studied from the third standard to the seventh standard; K.R. High School, from the eighth standard to the eleventh; and then Maharani Janaki Kunwar Inter College for the two years after his board exams, which was after the eleventh standard then.

Manoj didn't complain to his parents about the mental harassment he faced in school. Such things weren't given much importance then and were considered a part of the initiation process. The teachers were much respected, in fact feared. They couldn't be called out like today. The late Geeta Devi told me, 'Once our Manoj cried a lot and didn't want to return to the hostel. He kept crying till he reached the hostel gate but once inside the premises, he suddenly stopped crying.' Maybe, the kid knew he was on his own.

He felt helpless in the initial days in Bettiah because of the bullying, but unlike Gandhi, he had no one with him in this struggle.

The acting bug

The germ of acting caught up with Manoj in Bettiah. Kamini recalled: 'Manoj was in the sixth or seventh standard. Maa and

Babuji had come to Bettiah to meet us. They owned a small house there. I was supposed to go to the school on Monday, but I was in no mood to comply. Maa tried to reason, but when I refused, I was locked up in a room. Manoj didn't like this and pleaded with Maa to get me out. I was still not willing to go to school, but he kept pleading on my behalf. Eventually, Maa locked him up in my place, but he suddenly screamed and fell on the floor. Apparently, he was hit by a ladle. Maa got worried and ran towards him. The moment she pulled the ladle, Manoj got up laughing. We saw the first-hand demonstration of his acting capabilities that day.'

The late Radhakant Bajpayee also had a story in this context: 'We were at his school for the Guardian Day celebrations, where Manoj was playing the part of a village priest's sidekick. In a scene, the disciple (played by Manoj) brings a potful of sweets for the master. The pupil was supposed to look greedily at the sweets. A sweet somehow dropped on to the floor, and Manoj quickly grabbed and put it in his mouth. Everybody started laughing at his spontaneity. During the interval, I asked him if his act was part of the scene, and he said "no". He thought on his feet. I became suspicious about his intentions that day. I knew he was going to do something different.'

The play where Manoj did such effective improvision was called *Bemel Byaah* (Mismatched Marriage). Manoj acted in a couple of plays at K.R. High School, but he found an identity through poetry and recitation events, which won him much appreciation.

His friend Gyandev Mani Tripathi, who was a a year junior to him and a hostel mate, told me, 'He was better known in school for poetry recitations. His favourites were Dinkar's "Rashmirathi" and Harivansh Rai Bachchan's "Jo Beet Gayi So Baat Gayi".'

Manoj credits this school for the development of his personality. The school had a great environment. There were four big grounds, smart uniforms and everything else to get a village boy excited.

'It was the only school in that area with the infrastructure for hockey, lawn tennis, volleyball and other such sports,' Gyandev said. 'Manoj bhai and I were in the same hockey team, though he was better at football. Participating in games and taking a bath every day were compulsory. Sometimes, during winters, he would simply sprinkle a few drops of water on his body and step out of the bathroom. The hostel superintendent would scold him whenever he was caught acting.'

Manoj got addicted to films in this school. His favourites were films such as *Zanjeer* (1973), *Muqaddar ka Sikandar* (1978), *Shaan* (1980) and *Ek Duje ke Liye* (1980), which he watched several times.

In this context, Kamini told me, 'Manoj liked to take others to the cinema. We have seen *Bobby* [1973], *Bhabhi* [1991] and many other films together. Usually, our parents would be in Bettiah during the weekends and it was an occasion to watch films. Even when they were not in town and we wanted to watch films, we had to send a letter to Manoj through the gatekeeper of our hostel, and he would then take us to the theatre.'

It was at K.R. High School that Manoj first heard about NSD. His father believes that a school priest prompted his son to take up acting. Manoj, in an interview with Rajya Sabha TV's Irrfan, said, 'Acting was always there inside my heart and I wanted to do nothing else, but it wasn't seen as a respectable profession, so I kept the desire buried.'[14]

The Amitabh connection

K.R. High School gave Manoj a good start, but the next two years at Maharani Janki Kunwar College weren't really exciting. The college had a history. Maharani Janki Kunwar was Bettiah Estate's last queen. She was the second wife of the last king, Harendra Kishore Singh. The first wife, Shiv Ratan Kunwar, ascended the throne after the king's death on 26 March 1893, but she also passed away in 1896. Janki Kunwar was given the throne then. Later, the British declared her mentally unstable and took over the estate. The queen lived within the confines of the fort for a long time.

Even in Allahabad, the Bettiah Raj mansion is called 'Rani Bettiah's Kothi'. Since nobody lived there, the guards kept the doors of the palace mostly closed. Amitabh Bachchan spent his childhood in a nearby bungalow on 17 Clive Road. Amitabh and his friends had heard a lot about the mysterious palace and about Maharani Janki Kunwar. One day, when they couldn't contain their excitement and curiosity, they reached out to the gatekeeper and asked for the story in lieu of a *chawanni* (25 paise). Amitabh stole a chawanni from his mother's dressing table and gave it to the gatekeeper, but the kids were chased away. Later, Amitabh received an earful from his mother for the stolen money. He was even slapped for his antic. This incident is reported by Harivansh Rai Bachchan in his autobiography *Basere se Door*.[15]

It's a happy coincidence that Amitabh had so much impact on Manoj as an actor.

Bettiah had four cinema halls and all the shows would be covered within ten days. Sometimes, Manoj and the group of friends didn't even buy tickets and the usher would ask them for money during the shows. Occasional fights would then break out. Anish Ranjan, Manoj's school friend, told me, 'Once there was a knives-out in Janta Cinema. It was a fight with the usher, I guess.' Rajkumar Singh, another friend who was part of that fight, says, 'It happened during a show of *Naari* [1963]. It was an intense fight. All of us friends ran away to Gorakhpur and returned only after the case was forgotten, which was after some four or five days. We stayed at the Gorakhnath Temple and met Mahant Avaidyanath[16] as well.'

During this time, Manoj was getting restless as he wasn't able to find any outlet to satiate his hunger for acting. So Delhi seemed like a natural progression to him. He himself admitted later to me: 'I was quite restless in the two years of class eleventh and twelfth. There was no theatre scene in Bettiah and I didn't like it. I was also getting involved in the local gangs and politics. Because there was no creative outlet, the share of sprawl-brawl was increasing in life.'

There was a certain kind of aggression in Manoj's behaviour during his later days in Bettiah. It was an amalgamation of several things: the rebellious trait that he inherited from his father, the impact of films and peer pressure. One such incident happened when he returned to his village during a vacation. His father had taken a loan from a bank but missed paying a couple of instalments due to bad harvests. An officer from the bank reached their fields and reprimanded them for the delay in paying up. Manoj was there and it was a shocker for him. He somehow managed to control his anger and conceal his pain. No doubt the bank officer was rude, but what surprised and disappointed him the most was that his elder cousins who were present at the site didn't utter a single word in protest. 'I will throw money at these people when my time comes,' he later confided in a friend. And that day did come.

Bettiah and Manoj have an overarching relationship. They fulfil each other. It's his success in Bollywood that has given the local youngsters the hope to reach for the skies.

Chapter 4

Darling Delhi

'I was absolutely clueless in my initial days in Delhi. If I was asked to catch Bus No 302, I would keep staring at the vehicle's registration plate for hours.'

The distance between Bettiah and Delhi is some 1000-odd kilometres, but that distance seemed too daunting for Manoj. He had a dream, but no connections and contacts to help him make that dream a reality. He wanted to enrol at the NSD, which was in Delhi, and that came with its own set of challenges. Where to live, who to meet, how to survive?

It wasn't Manoj's first visit to Delhi. Earlier, he was there on a school trip. They even visited the Red Fort, Qutub Minar and other places of interest during the excursion. This is worth mentioning because, as per many media reports, Manoj first came to Delhi for his college admission, which in all probability was his third visit to the national capital. It was on his second visit to the city that Manoj decided to leave Bettiah and shift base to Delhi. The late Geeta Devi told me, 'When he asked me about entering the field of acting, I advised him to complete his graduation first. I was clear if he did his graduation, then he would know what's best for him.'

Delhi dreams

Manoj's younger sister Poonam recalls a conversation Manoj had with his mother: 'When Bhaiyya asked Maa for her permission to pursue acting, she asked him to complete his graduation first. It wouldn't be wise to leave his studies and pursue dramatics. Bhaiyya promised to go for his higher studies, though he knew theatre was his calling. That is what he wanted to do. Seeing his determination, Maa finally relented and allowed him to pursue his dream of becoming an actor.'

But the battle was only half won. He still needed a nod from his father. Radhakant might be a film fanatic, but it wasn't easy to convince him. Being an avid reader of film magazines, he was aware of the endless struggles an actor has to endure in the film industry. He recalled: 'Manoj said the academic session was quite delayed. A three-year course would take many more years. He wouldn't be able to study here, so he was going to Delhi for his BSc degree.'

Radhakant was sceptical about Manoj's choices because of the bad company he kept in Bettiah. He wasn't against the migration, but the real issue was the lack of money. 'I made it clear to my son the pressure I was in. I couldn't bear the expenses of the higher studies of six kids. He replied, "You do only what you can!"' Manoj told his father that he was going to Delhi to prepare for UPSC, though his father wanted him to pursue medical.

When Manoj landed in Delhi, the city was nothing short of a puzzle to him. It was during this time that his friend Ravindra Chaudhary came to his rescue. Ravindra's elder brother was pursuing graduation in commerce from Delhi University's Hansraj College. Ravindra told me, 'Manoj insisted that I should come along when I revealed I was going to Delhi the next day. I had a reservation, he didn't. He bought a ticket for the general compartment. I have read media stories about how Manoj hid in the toilet every time the travelling ticket examiner (TTE) came. Nothing of that sort happened. We used to travel in the sleeper class back then. He was running a fever that day. He slept on the berth, and I slept on the floor with the newspaper beneath.'

The whole TTE story spread in the media because Manoj himself talked about it in some interactions. He said in Rajya Sabha's programme *Guftagoo*, 'Narkatiaganj station was around 15 km from my village and very few trains arrived there. There wasn't any direct train to Patna. We had to change buses to reach Patna. The roads were in bad shape, and it took some ten to twelve hours to reach Patna. We boarded the Delhi-bound train from Patna. Ravindra Chaudhary had a reservation. I stayed awake throughout the night and travelled in the sleeper class without reservation, which was a crime. I kept moving in between compartments to avoid the TTE. I slept for a little while only when we reached Aligarh and the locals boarded the train.'

The two versions of passengers travelling together is kind of bizarre, but why would they lie? They didn't have any reason to say different things. When I watched the TV show 'Jeena Isi Ka Naam Hai', I found Ravindra Chaudhary saying the same thing in front of Manoj. So, what prompted Manoj to give a different version? Was it to make his struggles more romanticized? Can just one story cast doubts on the value of Manoj's struggles? So, I started the quest for the truth.

Manoj's younger sister Poonam told me, 'Babuji wanted Bhaiyya to be a doctor, he had even filled a form. He was supposed to go to Benares for the exam. I think he even started for it, but reached Delhi instead where he inquired about NSD. Then he broached the topic of acting with his mother and she put the graduation clause.'

Manoj probably hid from the TTE during this Delhi trip, and mixed up the two trips by mistake, or simply started repeating what was already said in the press conferences. He wasn't questioned after some time about this so-called trip in 1982–83.

There could be two stories about his pivotal Delhi trip, but it's established that he came to Delhi with one *sandook* (trunk), which he still has. He rode the Magadh Express with just Rs 500 in his pocket. He said in a BBC article published on 23 February 2004, 'Patna-Delhi trains stop around Tilak Bridge or Minto Bridge on not receiving green signal. Mine was stopped there as well. I peeped out of the window and saw Delhi. I was anxious about the National Capital. A kind of excitement was also there. I can't forget that image. A crowd of urban people was crossing the bridge beneath. I kept staring at the city and my grip over the window railing got stronger, and a voice came from my heart, "I will have a name in this city." '

University admission

It wasn't going to be easy in any way. The first hurdle was seeking admission in Delhi University. He didn't have enough marks in intermediate to get entry into the desired Ramjas College.

Ravindra was a badminton champion in Bihar University and thus he somehow managed to get admission in Ramjas College through the sports quota, but Manoj had to be content with Satyawati College and with a history honours. He said in an interview, 'Ravindra Chaudhary's elder brother tried his best to help me get admission in Ramjas College, but in vain.'

Manoj and Ravindra reached the hostel of Hansraj College where the latter's brother lived. They shifted to a flat in Mukherjee Nagar a week later. Ravindra remembered, 'We lived in flat number 1010 in Mukherjee Nagar. It had two rooms. Manoj and I stayed in one. My brother and Sanjeev Kumar, who later became the Rajya Sabha member, were in the other room. My brother took care of the kitchen expenses. I received Rs 550 in a money order from home, so we were not exactly facing any crunch. Manoj faced a financial crunch though. His money-orders also took four months to arrive, but life was like that and we shared resources.'

In an interview dated 12 October 2002, Manoj said, 'My pockets were empty. I wore Ravindra's clothes and used his belongings. Whenever I saw film posters at the nearby Batra Theatre, I dreamt of having my name on those posters.'[17]

Delhi wasn't a cakewalk, of course. Manoj himself admits being absolutely clueless during his initial days in Delhi. If he was asked to board Bus No. 302, he would keep staring at the vehicle's registration plate for hours! The actor went on to spend ten formative years in Delhi. These years transformed him as a person, as an actor and as a legend. These years are filled with stories that can serve as life lessons for those trying to make their dream a reality. A tale of struggle that perhaps won't fit into any prescribed slots. From failing to get admission in the NSD to becoming the brightest star in the world of theatre, Manoj saw many ups and downs in his life before finding his ultimate calling.

Chapter 5

Darling Delhi: First Acting Teacher

'The person, who upon reaching Delhi introduced me to the actor within me and made me realize the philosophies of Marx, Lenin and Mahatma Gandhi was Shamsul Islam.'

Upon his arrival in Delhi, Manoj's topmost agenda was to ensure admission in the NSD, but since his mother wanted him to complete his graduation first, he had three years to prepare for it. 'I didn't want to waste even a second,' he said.

The world of theatre

This enormous zeal took him to the Model Town office of Professor Shamsul Islam of Satyawati College. All the activities of the Nishant Natya Manch were controlled from here. Manoj describes his meeting in a candid way: 'I met Shamsul Islam and he included me in his group without any audition. I started coming to his office and taking part in official programmes.'

Manoj spent nearly three years with Nishant Natya Manch performing street plays. 'Manoj performed hundreds of plays with Nishant,' says Shamsul. 'We were in a play which had the anti-Sikh riots of 1984 as the backdrop. It was called *Sadharan Log* and it was staged at many places. He also had noteworthy roles in plays such as *Bhram ka Swang, Gaddhha* and *Vaastushashtra*.

Another play was *Sabse Sasta Gosht*. He had a prominent role and we staged it many times.'

Journalist Vinod Agnihotri, who was Manoj's colleague in Nishant, remembers, 'We staged *Sadharan Log* in Delhi for a full year. Manoj and I played Hindu and Sikh hardliners in this one. We also did *Girgit, Hawai Gole* and *Sabse Sasta Gosht*, and many other plays.'

These plays were conversation starters with the public. The interactions with the crowd led to focus group discussions among the members of the dramatic society. Shamsul emphasized the intellectual upbringing of the members. He said, 'Many colleagues have gotten slapped by me. Manoj must have been one of them.'

'Shamsul Islam was very particular about plays and we got slapped around sometimes, but nobody took it to heart,' Vinod Agnihotri confirms.

For Manoj, Nishant was like a school where he also learnt about life. 'Shamsul Islam was my first teacher. He taught me the importance of understanding society, polity and economics of our times to be an actor. One could become a great character only after developing a sense of social understanding. He also introduced me to progressive literature from all over the world. I became familiar with works in Russian, Chinese and other foreign languages.'.

Shamsul told me, 'From Baba Nagarjun to Shabana Azmi and Javed Akhtar, many prominent people came to the rehearsal ground of Nishant. It was important for our students to read everything from Nagarjun and Chekhov to Gorky and Tolstoy. Our library had many books. Students from the Hindi belt usually avoided the English books, but Manoj borrowed them and circled the parts he didn't understand so that he could get clarity on them.'

English, what English?

Within three months of landing in Delhi, Manoj understood the importance of English. 'Delhi elites spoke English, and

I knew I couldn't interact with them without knowing English. I also thought of maintaining some distance with the Hindi- and Bhojpuri-speaking people around me. I thought of a way. I befriended some Nigerian and Kenyan boys. We spoke in broken English but slowly started catching up. People I lived with would ask me to speak a few lines in English and then they would laugh at my accent, but I kept marching ahead. With time, my English got better.'

The three years at Nishant were life changing for Manoj as he understood the value of collaboration. He came out of his own complexes and started a new journey. He said on BBC Hindi. com, 'I hailed from a traditional Brahmin family in Bihar. I had years of rigid societal norms inside me. I was made aware about casteism, feudalism and elitism since birth. I was told there was a washerman in the times of Lord Ram, so there should be one even now. The existence of upper and lower castes is not unusual. Shamsul's proximity changed my mindset. I came out of my time's paradoxes and many of my contradictions were challenged. During this era of evolution, I found a worldview. Staging plays against social distortions and economic unevenness and discussing the country's current political scenarios became part of my daily routine.'[18]

Manoj credits Shamsul for his transformation. 'The person, who upon reaching Delhi introduced me to the actor within me, and made me realize the philosophies of Marx, Lenin and Gandhi was Shamsul Islam.'

Shamsul reciprocated the feeling. 'Manoj had this incredible urge to learn, and he was a quick learner. He never said no to any work. I carried a heavy bag whenever we travelled around 30km for plays and he always insisted on carrying it. He was courteous and liked by all.

'Once we went to a restaurant and ordered corn soup, it was the cheapest. When it was served, Manoj asked, "Isn't this *maand* [starch]?" We still have a good laugh remembering it.'

'His speciality was remembering long dialogues with much ease,' Vinod Agnihotri corroborates.

Manoj was close to Shamsul's family. Their daughter Shivi was quite fond of him and called him 'Chacha'. He also loved her a lot.

Manoj made many friends at Nishant, and among them Bharat Acharya was special. Bharat owned a gas agency and took care of Manoj's well-being as well. He passed away following a cardiac arrest on 24 January 2019.

Manoj did the first year of his graduation at Satyawati and managed to get transferred to Ramjas with some help from his friends and teachers. He kept doing plays at Nishant and Ramjas simultaneously. These included *The Comedy of Errors* and *An Enemy of the People*, among others. The latter was the first play in which he got the lead role. He also performed in many shows in Hindu College. When they were looking for a heroine, many girls from Hindu College were willing to audition for the role, but they weren't ready to embrace Manoj in a scene in the play as their parents were expected to come and watch the play. They finally managed to find an actress in Indraprastha College who was willing to play the role. She had no qualms about kissing on stage as well. Desh Deepak, the director of the play, wanted to cast Ashish Vidyarthi in the lead, but Ashish turned down the offer. Manoj saw Ashish performing for the first time in Ramjas and was really impressed with his command over Hindi as well as English.

Manoj parted ways with Nishant after graduation. Shamsul never sensed Manoj's strong leaning towards films. 'He had a great eagerness for theatre. I believed this is what he wanted to do for the rest of his life. I gave him the example of Indian People's Theatre Association [IPTA] which failed its mission when its prominent actors started working in Bollywood and left the ideology behind. Probably that is why he never talked about moving to Mumbai.'

It seems Shamsul's ultra-left ideology was also a reason behind Manoj's drift. Manoj wrote in a column for the BBC, 'The person who gave me Shamsul Islam's name also told me about his left leaning and theatre background. Truth be told, I wasn't really aware about the ideological differences.'[19]

Shamsul's involvement with the Naxalbari movement was a known thing. He also did guerilla plays during the Emergency.[20] He admits his relationship with Naxal groups. 'I got married after the Emergency ended. Then we did our first show at Azadpur Municipal Market on 28 September 1977. It was *Girgit*. After working for a while on such plays, we formed Nishant, our drama company.'

Nishant still carries the same ideology. 'We have expelled famous actors from Nishant after knowing that their wives have fasted for a son, or they have been a part of weddings where dowry was demanded,' says Shamsul.

More than a theatre group, Nishant operated like a political agency. The plays were given specific political flavours. This might have made Manoj uncomfortable, and then there was the dream of NSD too.

Shamsul's expectations from Manoj died when he left the group. He told me, 'Manoj is a part of the rat race now. He should have returned to his village because he was famous and could have raised money.'

Manoj has also talked about returning to his roots, but not every wish turns into reality!

Anyway, it's easier said than done.

Chapter 6

Darling Delhi: The NSD Dream

'I failed and it was a heart-wrenching experience because I didn't have a plan B. I confined myself to a room. Weird thoughts persisted, and one of them was of suicide.'

The NSD is the Mandi House-based Mecca of theatre artists. Om Shivpuri, Mohan Maharishi, Ram Gopal Bajaj, B.L. Chopra, Uttara Baokar, Surekha Sikri, Balraj Pandit, Devendra Raj Ankur, Suhasini Kale, Rajendra Gupta, Manohar Singh, Jyoti Deshpande, Om Puri, Naseeruddin Shah, Bhanu Bharti, Rohini Hattangadi, Raj Babbar, Rajit Kapur, Pankaj Kapur, Sabina Mehta, Virendra Razdan, Anang Desai, Anita Kanwar, Anupam Kher, Raghubir Yadav, Dolly Ahluwalia, Alok Nath, Deepa Shahi, Himani Bhatt Shivpuri, Seema Biswas and Avtar Singh. These are names who were already famous in the theatre world before Manoj sat for his NSD entrance exam. Many names like Naseeruddin Shah, Om Puri and Raj Babbar were already big in the film world, and their success was spoken about even in villages.

Since Radhakant was an avid reader of film magazines, Manoj must have heard about such stories from his father. There are different versions of the story of how his fascination with the NSD began. He has cited the *Ravivar* magazine at one place. In the Rajya Sabha TV interview, he said, 'I had heard a lot about the National School of Drama. It was mentioned in Naseeruddin Shah or Raj Babbar's interviews. There were other graduates also. While reading them, it seems this is where I should be! I wasn't born in a big city or a place with proximity to acting. I knew I had to learn acting in an organized way. I had the eagerness to learn. That's why I had boarded the Delhi-bound train and nurtured the dream of NSD.'[21]

The elusive dream

Manoj sat for the NSD entrance exam for the first time in 1986. He was hopeful. He had a rich theatre experience of almost three years. He was a lot more confident as an actor now. He also had a better command over his diction. While living the NSD dream, he met another zealous youngster—Vijay Raj. Their common friend—Kavita Vaidya—introduced them during a play in the basement of the Shri Ram Centre for Performing Arts. They clicked instantly. Vijay was a graduate of Banaras Hindu University and wanted to get into the NSD. 'We started spending time together. We met in the morning and sat in the NSD library during the day for preparation,' says Vijay.

Not to be confused with the actor Vijay Raj, this one is better recognized as a writer, though he has acted in films like Vishal Bhardwaj's *Makdee*.

They had another friend—Tigmanshu Dhulia, who according to Vijay, was full of confidence. 'Don't know how, but Tigmanshu was damn sure about getting admission in NSD.' Well, Tigmanshu was the only one to get admission out of the three. Manoj and Vijay couldn't clear even the written test.

Manoj went into a shock; he never anticipated such a result. 'I failed, and it was a heart-wrenching experience because I didn't have a plan B. I confined myself to a room. Weird thoughts persisted, and one of them was of suicide. Friends came to my support and inspired me to leave the failure behind.'

NSD could have solved two fundamental issues for Manoj. The first was to learn the craft from the masters of the game. When he watched Piyush Mishra's play *Hamlet* in 1985, he was mesmerized. 'Piyush's *Hamlet* was quite a hit. I had seen two shows and I aspired to be an artist like him. When I watched his lyrics and singing, I wondered whether I would have to be born twice to be like him.'

Many NSD students established themselves even before they completed their studies and this is what Manoj wanted too.

The other benefit he would derive was to dedicate his time solely to theatre as the world outside the campus wasn't particularly benevolent. Manoj, in an NSD event, once said, 'There are battles outside, like there is a house owner [waiting] once you return after rehearsals. There is the worry of cooking food, travelling in crowded buses and many other struggles. NSD saves you from all that. Your only work is honing craft. I wanted to learn like this.'

Once the NSD dream was shattered, he was back to the harsh realities of life. One day, he came to know of a theatre workshop group called Sambhav through some his classmates. Actors such as Seema Pahwa, Manoj Pahwa and Virendra Saxena were part of that group. 'Sambhav was considered the biggest group of the Delhi theatre circuit. They were starting a one-year training course. The fee was Rs 2500. The plan was for NSD graduates to teach there, which was very encouraging. I somehow borrowed the required money needed to join the group. I was so excited about it that I didn't take even a day off from the workshop.'

Vijay Raj was with Manoj in this workshop, and they completed it with utmost sincerity. Vijay recalled, 'During that time, there was a government-sponsored cultural event titled "Apna Utsav". Devendra Raj Ankur was our teacher, and Bhanu Bharti was the in-charge of the Rajasthan zone. He asked Devendra-ji for two volunteers. Ankur-ji had seen how two resourceless, but obsessed, boys were dedicated to theatre. He suggested our names. We were assigned the work of queueing up all the actors before going on the stage. This seven-day job earned us Rs 2500, it was like winning a lottery. We partied at a dhaba the day we were paid. Daal-roti-sabzi-makhkhan. This money sailed us through for some days.'

'It was my first job,' says Manoj.

Such rosy days were not in abundance. Sometimes Manoj didn't have enough money to buy a bus ticket. A bus trip to Manoj's rented place from Mandi House cost Re 1. Whenever they had Rs 8–10 extra, it called for a celebratory film viewing at Pragati Maidan's Shankuntalam Theatre. 'A ticket cost Rs 2, so Rs 4 went into it, and the rest was utilized in purchasing a samosa each,' says Vijay Raj.

To save money, Manoj took admission in a Pali language course in Delhi University, because it enabled him to get a DTC bus pass of Rs 12.50 for a month. 'My mind was not in the class. The only thing that I wanted was to learn acting. When the Sambhav workshop kicked off, I discontinued the Pali language course.'

After dedicating a full year to Sambhav, Manoj was back at the same juncture. This time, he was even more serious for the NSD entrance. He started preparing for the NSD with all sincerity. He spoke about his obsession at an NSD event. 'You work with the famous and revered directors from all over the world here. We had to find them and request them to include us in their plays.'

But unfortunately, he failed for the second time as well. He was depressed for a couple of days, but he did not give up hope. Meanwhile, his acting journey started taking some shape. He worked with different groups in 1987–88. He worked with Sambhav on a play based on Kashinath Singh's *Apna Morcha*. He also worked with Devendra Raj Ankur. He also did Narendra Mohan's play based on Kabir's life. He made the best of every

opportunity that came his way. Manoj also started taking lessons
in the Chhau folkdance. 'It's a semi-classical dance. I trained for
almost three hours every morning in the open-air theatre. This
training went on for close to four years.'

Chhau is a type of dance drama that is traditionally performed
in West Bengal, Bihar and Odisha. The three branches of Chhau
originated in Seraikela (Bihar), Purulia (West Bengal) and
Mayurbhanj (Odisha). Fast lyrical dialogues, expressions and the
calculated use of space are its highlights. The other speciality of this
dance form is the use of masks; in fact, the gods and demons are
differentiated through masks. Actor Vineet Kumar's first memory
of Manoj Bajpayee is of a Chhau student. 'I did theatres for years in
Patna. Then I reached NSD. I was older than others. One morning,
there was a light shower, and I saw a lungi-clad boy learning the
dance steps, completely oblivious to his surroundings. I would
never forget this visual of discipline and dedication.'

Many of Manoj's friends had to go for Chhau dance training
because of him. Filmmaker Anil Chaudhary, who was once
Manoj's roommate, said that Manoj's body movements were
good. 'He told us his teacher would start classes if there were three
or four students. We had to oblige. That also meant waking up
at six in the morning. One day, we met Safdar Hashmi, and he
also joined us. One day, Guruji scolded Safdar for not getting the
steps. To which, he replied: "*Mera aangan tedha hai* [My courtyard
is uneven]". He had an impeccable sense of humour.'

Despite failing to secure a seat in NSD, Manoj was well
known within the campus and among the famous directors. Even
then he failed for the third time. Vijay Raj also failed. They sat
in the NSD lawn and talked at length about their future. They
thought of making peace with their fate and moving on.

'Politics was at its peak at NSD in those days. I was also
a victim, to such an extent that I went on a one-year leave in
1986,' says former NSD professor Robin Das. 'I was harassed
because I wore slippers and mingled with the students, and what

not! Manoj was also a victim to this politics. Those who were responsible for giving admission gave the logic that if they have to take students from Bihar in then they should be taking the ones coming from villages. Some kids from rural backgrounds come to Delhi, learn theatre and then apply to get admission. This was a bizarre logic. Actually, they were scared of the talented lot because they could question wrong practices. They didn't want that.'

'Being rejected became a habit by the third time,' says Manoj. 'Professor Tripurari Sharma was surprised to see me keep trying despite failing. The struggles outside the campus make the process of learning acting difficult. I wanted to get into NSD for uninterrupted training. It didn't happen, but it instilled the virtue of hard work in me. Also, I made extensive use of the NSD library.'

After repeated rejections, Manoj finally decided to let go of the NSD dream. But it was so deeply engrained in his subconscious that he couldn't forget it even when he was working with the legendary theatre personality Barry John's action group. He sat for the NSD entrance for the fourth time and failed yet again!

Even Manoj doesn't know where he fell short. He does know that when he didn't get into NSD, he doubled his efforts. He prepared himself so much that when it came to acting, he could stand up to any actor on the Delhi stage. However, NSD's rejection always bothered him.

Brecht to the rescue

In the aftermath of mixed emotions, Manoj was contacted by Robin Das, a well-known theatre director. The year 1988 was almost drawing to an end. During that time, a theatre festival was being held in Pragati Maidan where Das staged Bertolt Brecht's *Drums in the Night*. Manoj, Vijay and Lovleen were part of this play.

'I had worked with Manoj in Sambhav,' Robin told me. 'He was very hard-working, and he had gained fame by the time

Drums in the Night was staged. He was also working with Barry at that time. I think I commented on something during rehearsals. As a result, when I went to wish him luck before the first show, he got cold feet. He felt that I was not liking his acting. I asked him to not take directors so seriously. I assured him that he was indeed brilliant and that he was the heavy lifter of the play. He had to dance in a scene, and he was playing a character whose girlfriend was getting married to somebody else. He did such an impromptu dance that the scene became incredible. My play and another NSD play were being staged simultaneously. I went to watch that play as well. We did three shows of the play. I sanctioned leave to NSD students to watch the play. This was for them to understand how to create a perfect character. While watching the play, I also realized the gap between theories and its practical manifestations.'

Manoj's friend Nikhil Verma is of the opinion that Manoj's character was the main attraction of that play: 'On the last day before the show, Robin Das said he has invited first, second and third year NSD students to watch the play. It was like a case study for them. A long question-and- answer session followed the show. We weren't able to leave before midnight. We started on foot towards our Railway Colony house. There was a strange confidence in his walk, one had to see it to believe it. We all were up till 3–4 a.m., which was unusual for Manoj. I had never seen him sleep more peacefully.'

Nikhil works in the advertisement industry and is based in Mumbai.

It must have been a huge moral victory for Manoj. After all, his talent was validated by the professor and students at the same institute that rejected him four times. It was also the acceptance of a world he had created in his mind and soul. How much acting mattered to him can be understood from what he had said about the national capital: 'I was very confined in Delhi. I didn't even go to see the Qutub Minar.' He is now, of course, a prominent face at NSD as a visiting faculty.

Chapter 7

Darling Delhi: The Second Acting Guru

'Barry taught me the nitty-gritties of theatre in a short span, which would have taken years otherwise. He took me to the nooks and corners of society. My problems dwarfed in front of those experiences.'

After failing to qualify in the NSD entrance exam multiple times, Manoj found solace in Barry John's group. His camaraderie with Barry deeply impacted his life. Barry gave him the mantra for success—stop talking, start doing.

Barry John came to India from Britain in a youth exchange programme in 1968. This era belonged to the hippie culture, but Barry maintained his distance and started off as an English teacher in Bengaluru. He was a trained theatre artist and came to Delhi as part of a group named Yatrik. Following a request from NSD's first director Ebrahim Alkazi, Barry designed a workshop. He worked with NSD till 1973 but was forced to part ways due to the politics in the campus. He then started Theatre Action Group (TAG). He received support from legends of theatre such as Siddhartha Basu, Roshan Seth, Lillete Dubey, Mira Nair, Ravi Dubey, Manohar Singh, Khalid Tyabji, Pamela Rooks, Surekha Sikri and Pankaj Kapur.

Despite being British, spending fifty years in India made Barry as Indian as Indian can be. Meeting him turned out to be a turning point in Manoj's career as this collaboration made him a better actor and also gave him a sense of direction. Language wasn't a barrier despite Barry not knowing enough Hindi and Manoj having workable knowledge of English.

Actor Raghubir Yadav was the one who took Manoj to Barry. 'He was very sad after failing to get into NSD for the third time,' says Raghubir. 'I remember he was sitting in NSD's park. When he told me about his failed attempts at the NSD entrance, I told him it's a good thing. He looked at me surprised and wondered why I said so. "A new thing can't be created unless something old gets broken. So, you consider yourself lucky," I told him. He asked what he should do, and it was then that I told him about Barry and the play I was doing with him. I asked him to come along for the workshop. "Your career will be set if you get selected," I assured him. His eyes were filled with hunger. When I went for chai that evening at the NSD square, he came along.'

What's interesting is that Manoj had been wanting to work with Barry even before their first meeting. Manoj had in fact talked to his assistant, Sanjay Sujitabh, regarding this. 'I met him [Manoj] for the first time during the casting workshop of TAG's play *Baghdad ka Ghulam*, which was an adaptation of the Italian playwright Carlo Goldoni's *The Servant of Two Masters*. He was just a college student with poor English, but in his eyes, I saw the hunger for better work,' says Barry.

Manoj was wearing a kurta and was a little apprehensive during their first meeting. In contrast, when Shah Rukh Khan met Barry for the first time during an audition in Lady Shri Ram, he was confident and told Barry that he wanted to be a part of whatever was happening there. It might be due to the difference in their cultural backgrounds: Manoj studied in a small town, spoke Hindi, wore simple clothes. Shah Rukh, on the other hand, studied at a convent school in Delhi and was adept at English.

Raghubir Yadav had translated *Baghdad ka Ghulam* into Hindi and was playing the lead role in it. Manoj was cast as an inn owner named Rehmatullah. 'Raghubir Yadav was definitely in the centre,' says Barry. 'His understanding of folk arts helped him get the character right. He danced, sang, loved and resealed the envelope with saliva. He improvised while breaking the fourth wall. That is how he played the character of a servant for two of his masters staying in the same motel without them knowing about each other. Manoj played the manager, which meant constant interaction with Yadav. The play had a famous scene where the servant serves food to both masters simultaneously. It was preceded by a funny scene with the masters discussing the lunch menu. Manoj played a homosexual character, who was tired of Yadav for mispronouncing his famous Arabic dish and added dimensions to it.'

'Truth be told Manoj gained three years of experience in that one play!' says Yadav.

The *Statesman* assessed Manoj's performance as being at par with Raghubir. 'That character got me [Manoj] fame. Some critics wrote that if anybody could play Raghubir's role in the Delhi theatre circuit, it was me. It was a big compliment because there wasn't anyone better than Raghubir Yadav at that time. I wanted to be like him.'

The play was a hit. Sanjay Sujitabh says, 'The first staging of *Baghdad ka Ghulam* took place in Delhi's Kamani Auditorium. Barry sir maintained a unique record that he wouldn't do more than seven shows of any play howsoever big it might be. But this one had twenty-one shows in Delhi and Kolkata in three months.'

Rituraj, Divya Seth, Deepika Deshpande and Shah Rukh also essayed roles in the play. Shah Rukh played a prince named Khalid, but the two people who received the most accolades were none other than Raghubir and Manoj.

Barry witnessed Manoj's latent talent from close quarters. He also taught Manoj life skills. Manoj met Shah Rukh, Divya and others during the workshop of the play.

Initially, Manoj was anxious for a couple of weeks. Barry either spoke English or kept quiet. Nor did he look at anyone while speaking. There would be a diary in front of him, in which he would take notes. Manoj felt out of place as there was a bit of a communication gap. Half of the boys were from South Delhi. They were rich boys from well-to-do families. Only three-fourths were from middle and lower middle-class backgrounds. Barry understood the gap that existed between people from different cultures and backgrounds. He sensed the tension and tried to defuse it by including sports in the curriculum. It was a good icebreaker. 'Today I understand the value of football, and any sport in fact. Later we—Shah Rukh and Ravindra Sahu and a few others— became good friends and the gap was bridged. We performed in a Hindi play and my work in it was much appreciated.'

It was a phase of transition for Manoj and he was trying his best to cope with the change in his surroundings. Despite no steady flow of income, he marched on. After all, hunger never waits for you to succeed first. Shah Rukh had a car even back then in which he used to drop his colleagues home.

Manoj received an offer of collaboration from Barry during the staging of *Baghdad Ka Ghulam*. 'Barry called me before the last show of *Baghdad Ka Ghulam* and asked me if I wanted to work with him. He agreed to pay me Rs 1200 a month. He also promised to train me and give me work as an assistant. I confided in him about my dream of getting into NSD, to which he said, "I will personally give you the kind of training you need for that. I have never done it for anyone else, but I think it will be a good change and exciting as well. I am sure I will enjoy working with you." I haven't seen this kind of attachment, energy and dedication towards his craft.'

Barry told me, 'Sometimes hunger gets very real and immediate, but even that didn't stop Manoj from giving it his 110 per cent. There were times when his expressions gave away glimpses of restless energy, and that only made his presentation more noteworthy.'

'My [Manoj's] work was to organize the workshop and also train children.'

'Manoj started out as an assistant. I can't remember how many of the projects were together and how many were his solo projects. He did one workshop for SOS Children's Villages of India, Greenfields, for which he had to attend a summer camp in Saat Taal. The play we did with the kids was called *Bhagwan ki Adalat*,' Barry recalls. 'He was also my assistant during the classes organised for Hauz Khas's Spastic Society of Northern India. We did a play there titled *Talaash*. We also worked in an ambitious project with the students of Lodhi Estate's Sardar Patel School, which was staged at Shri Ram Centre. He did an independent workshop for the summer camp of South Delhi's Birla Vidya Niketan in which the issues related to the school and parents were shown. It was titled *Chakravyuh*. One of the most challenging plays we performed was the one we did with the kids who lived in and around the New Delhi Railway Station. It was an educational and social project named *Nukkad*. These kids narrated stories about their lives and the group improvised them. This was the reflection of issues we all were facing. Another play titled *Jeevan ki Gaadi* was being planned with Manoj and Loveleen Mishra in the lead. It was staged at Triveni Kala Sangam's open-air theatre to make the audience understand the plight of the kids living on roads. Manoj and Loveleen played various characters in this.'

Manoj was so serious about the play that he used to think of details in child actors' work. His friend and journalist Rajesh Joshi says, 'There was a play by street kids outside ITO's Express Building. There was a four- or five-year old girl and a six- or seven-year-old boy in it. Manoj dressed them as tourists, with hats and shades. It was a shopping scene based in Connaught Place. Manoj was really tense as the kids were performing on the streets. He was biting his nails and appeared restless. He was worried that the children would forget their dialogues. He was very involved in the project.'

All these activities were teaching him the intricacies of art. 'Whatever Barry gave him, Manoj did. He used to ask Barry for more work and feedback after rehearsals. He too took notes like Barry sir,' says Sanjay Sujitabh.

Barry taught him that plays are a thing of fewer words and more expressions. 'Barry taught me the nitty-gritties of theatre in a short span, which would have taken years otherwise. He took me to the nooks and corners of society. My problems dwarfed in front of those experiences. I haven't seen a teacher like Barry John. He didn't handhold me nor was he very strict. He was in fact very soft spoken. He would devise a system, a method, and then make you a part of it, but you have to be your own guide.'

Manoj was hard-working and disciplined and Barry's guidance gave him direction. 'I would reach Barry's at around seven in the morning and return home late at night.'

Nikhil was privy to Manoj's extraordinary dedication. 'Manoj was very happy working with Barry. He was so disciplined that every night he slept at the right time to wake up much in advance to reach Barry on time. He knew he couldn't give it his best if he was tired, so he followed his routine religiously. He would head off to sleep even if other people were sitting and chatting in his room. He would react sharply if someone tried to wake him up from his sleep. After Safdar Hashmi's death, some theatre and Jana Natya Manch people organized an event outside Shri Ram Centre in his memory. A friend, well . . . basically one of Manoj's friends, had come for the event. We asked him to stay with us. We returned at eleven in the evening, and asked Manoj to wake up and meet his old friend. When he didn't respond, I pulled his blanket, and he got furious. It almost came to blows. Also, he would never go out in the morning on an empty stomach. There was a Hanuman

Temple near our place where you could find doodh-jalebi. He would eat that and get to work.'

Manoj Bajpayee lived in house number E-65 in Railway Colony near Mandi House. As mentioned earlier, he would get home from work quite late in the evening. Once he got back home, he was surprised to find some thirty-odd boys sleeping in his house. Vineet Kumar was present that day. 'I can't forget that scene even if I try. He was shocked upon entering the room. He pulled the sheet from many boys' faces to figure out if any outsider was there who can be sent out, but all were acquaintances, and all of them were in deep sleep. He somehow made a place for himself. Now when I recall this, I realize how happy we were. There were difficulties, but we weren't bitter.'

Manoj faced challenges head-on while working with Barry, and one such moment was when he was supposed to do a play in France and in French. Manoj's friend and producer Ashok Purang has this to say: 'Students of India and France collaborated for a play to support cultural exchange. Some Delhi Public School students, who were taught French, participated in it. Similarly, the French school kids studied English. The backdrop of the play was a situation in which a plane carrying Indian and French nationals crash into an island. There was an old man among the passengers, and his role was essayed by Manoj. The language of the play was English in India, so it was managed, but it was also scheduled to happen in French in France. Manoj was expected to deliver a page-long dialogue at the end. Though the French Embassy deputed a French teacher for Manoj, he insisted on learning from me. So I taught him for an hour every day. I had some experience of theatre and understood the basics of it. He worked on his speech and diction for close to fourteen hours a day! He rehearsed like crazy. When the play was finally staged in a big auditorium in France, a renowned French director who was in the audience was so impressed by his performance that he invited Manoj to join his repertory.'

This trip to France was his first air flight and he was anxious throughout the entire ten-hour journey. His fear of heights didn't help either. In fact, Manoj is not fond of flying even now. But before making the journey, another fear gripped him. Manoj was afraid that he would not have enough money to fund this trip. 'I didn't have the money to buy dollars before going to France. Ashok helped me with managing the money. The late Amit Bhatia also pitched in. I eventually managed to have 500 dollars. We stayed at a French actor's house. That two-month travel taught me a lot. My horizon extended and my perspective changed. I was encouraged by the audience's response.'

Manoj narrated an interesting story related to this plane journey on *The Kapil Sharma Show*. He wasn't aware that passengers were served liquor on international flights, so he kept saying "no" to the hostess. He wasn't sure whether he would have to pay for it!

The hectic lifestyle had started to show on Manoj's face and Barry, upon realizing it, advised him to take a break to visit his village. Manoj took up the offer. When he returned from his trip, Manoj was invigorated and charged up with double the energy. And to top that, Barry made him even happier by increasing his allowance to Rs 1800 a month. But of course that came with new responsibilities. Manoj was no longer confined to just the training. He was allowed to work outside. Barry's doors of course were always open for him.

But Manoj began to realize that his goal was to become an actor, not a director.

Chapter 8

Darling Delhi: Act One

'Netua *completely established me. It was very successful. It changed the rules of theatre. People watched it not once but ten times.'*

The Act One Theatre Group is quite respected in the Delhi theatre circuit and it couldn't have scaled great heights without Manoj Bajpayee. The group was supported by many famous personalities who had joined hands because of their love for theatre. The group demands a separate book in itself but consider this an attempt to tell its story with Manoj in the middle.

The first scene would open in the back lawn of NSD where some Mandi House regulars played football. The year was 1989. One day, the ball hit a culture veteran, and everything changed after that. Anish Ranjan, one of the founders of Act One, says, 'The path to Kathak Centre went through the lawn. We had a rule that we would stop the game if anybody would cross that path. Birju Maharaj was crossing the path on that fateful day. He didn't appreciate theatre and NSD students because he taught at the Kathak Centre and the boys looked lustily at the girls of the centre. One day, Rajender Nautiyal kicked the ball which hit Birju Maharaj. He looked at us seething in anger, but we continued playing. Next day, a wall was erected around the lawn. Then the idea of doing plays came to our mind. N.K. Sharma wanted to stage *Marisa*, but it was short, so it was decided we would find another play.'

Nikhil took Ratan Verma's story 'Netua', which was published in the *Hans* magazine, to the group. Nikhil says, 'Liquor would arrive after the football game, and close to twenty people didn't mind drinking. We were all frustrated, and we all had the habit of reading. When I told them about *Netua*, everyone agreed it could be a good play.'

'One day, during a game of football, Manoj suddenly offered to collaborate as an actor and a director. I promised to work with him only if something great came our way,' says N.K. Sharma.

Netua was a good script, but the lead role was very complex for any ordinary actor's sake. Sharma says, 'I would have rejected the story if I hadn't known Manoj. I knew his capabilities. I told him we are going to rock this one. But I warned him that he would have to work really hard and change his entire body language for this role. He would have to perform the *launda* dance, a rural dance where males dress as females, to which he readily agreed. He was willing all the way to get into the character.'

Sharma was a Bombay-return. He was the chief assistant director on Shashilal K. Nair's *Angaar* but stepped down after creative differences. He was looking for a breakthrough. 'Bihar was in the background of the story. I had no experience of that life, so I picked up two people: Vijay Bhai (Manoj's roommate) and Anish. I asked them to create scenes as per my mould. Everyone had something to contribute when discussions over the script began. Manoj was quite active in them, so I asked him to join the writing team. It was initially difficult for him, but he managed,' says Sharma.

Eventually, the script was ready, with Vijay Raj, Anish Ranjan and Manoj Bajpayee sharing the writing credits.

There was indeed a creative energy to the lawn behind NSD, but to rehearse, they needed a bigger space.. The group of amateurs didn't have enough cash to hire a rehearsal place. Anish, who had the privilege of knowing a Bihar MP, Dhanraj Singh, came handy. His government house was utilized for rehearsals.

Manoj went to extreme lengths to put soul into his character. Pushkar Sinha, who gave music in the initial editions of *Netua*, said, 'Manoj practised like there's no tomorrow. He would reach the studio at around two-thirty in the afternoon if rehearsals were to start from four in the evening. Birju Maharaj's disciple Madhukar Anand taught him dance. I would sit behind the harmonium. Manoj had to work extra on his body's tensile quotient. The dance practice preceded the actual rehearsal.'

Manoj practised dance in the mornings as well. He took on the challenge with all his might. Rajeev Gaur, who was stationed backstage in *Netua*, says, 'Manoj practised at home as well. He had to perform with a lehenga-choli on and had to act in a feminine manner and pick up womanly mannerisms; all this was difficult. He took his role so seriously that at one point he actually started talking like the character in real life, much to the amusement of his friends.'

Actor Gajraj Rao also has a story about Manoj's obsession with characters: 'One day, during the staging of the play, just before the last scene, Manoj was sitting in one corner of the green room, deeply engrossed in his thoughts. Our friend Umesh entered the space and started joking around to keep the mood light before the emotional climax. Manoj screamed at him after almost ten minutes. Umesh was startled and his eyes became moist.'

Netua is about a guy who cross-dresses in weddings for money. He has a wife too. He has to put up with economical and physical exploitations by the village's powerful people, but his threshold of tolerance gets breached.

The group also debated about the banner under which the play would be performed. The process of getting a new group registered was complicated. 'A different banner was needed for the play. Atul Kumar was a close friend of mine. He said he has a group registered by the name Act One, but it wasn't active. He wanted me to take it on and in return I offered him to join the group. Next morning, he came with around five people and a certificate to our rehearsal. That is how Act One was officially formed, in 1989, but the first show was performed only next year,' says Sharma.

There was a new group, but their pockets were still empty. Some friends collected money and booked the Shri Ram Centre for three shows. Some handmade posters were circulated too. It was publicized in and around Mandi House. Most of the costumes were managed by the performers since there was no budget to buy them. Even during the time of the financial crunch, Varsha Agnihotri, who played Netua's wife, was paid. Probably she was the only actor to be paid. 'I was around nineteen or twenty at that time. I met Gajraj Rao during a play at Lady Shriram College and joined Act One. I asked for some remuneration when I was offered the role. I was probably given Rs 150–200,' she recalls.

'*Netua* turned out to be a game changer. No other group had managed to pull off such a flawless first show. Manoj became a theatre star overnight after *Netua*. Many of NSD's faculty members and established artists congratulated us the next day,' says Vijay Raj.

There was a huge line of spectators waiting to get tickets to the second show. Another Act One member Arun Kumar Kalra says, 'The crowd was overwhelming. I watched only one show because I was made to sit at the ticket counter.'

An interesting incident happened during the third show. The electricity supply faltered right before the interval and everyone's face turned pale for a moment. Gajraj Rao, who played a small role in the play, shares this anecdote: 'When the lights went out, nobody knew how to react. I don't know what came upon me, but I reached on to the stage and started speaking impromptu. I think it was a story about a village with no electricity, or something similar. We realized work can be done in the dark as well.'

Meanwhile, Anubhav Sinha also got on to the stage with a candle in his hand and made some announcements to pacify the audience. The play then started in the candlelight. The electricity returned after a while.

There was another incident during one of the shows. The set collapsed during another show. Manoj was delivering his dialogues in the last scene of the play when the set suddenly broke with a thud. But his awareness was such that he connected this event with the script.

Three shows of *Netua* was staged in September 1990 and a few more over the next month. All were hits. The shows took place in the basement. It was such a hit that audiences of English plays too started trickling in.

Manoj's friend Gyandev Mani Tripathi had also seen the play at the Shri Ram Centre: 'The last act was mesmerizing—the part where Netua removes his anklets and throws them away, demanding equality. It was hair-raising. I remember that Rajendra Yadav, the editor of *Hans* magazine, had come for one of the shows and he was left awestruck by Manoj's performance.'

Manoj is aware of the critical role *Netua* played in his journey. '*Netua* completely established me. It was very successful. It changed the rules of theatre. People watched it not once but ten times. No other character has given me more happiness than this one. I would rehearse for sixteen hours. I learnt kathak for my role and achieved what I wanted through my performance.'

In the meantime, a 19-year-old boy became aware of Manoj's talent through *Netua*, and he was none other than Anurag Kashyap. He told me how stunned he was after watching the play. He wasn't aware of Manoj Bajpayee at that time. In fact, he went backstage to meet him. 'Everyone in the greenroom wanted to meet Baju bhai [Manoj's close friends call him Baju Bhai],' says Anurag Kashyap.

Manoj was active in theatre for close to six years, but *Netua* was the breakthrough performance he was looking for. Its popularity transcended boundaries. The late Radhakantji told me, 'My nephew, who was studying medicine, came home with some of his friends. They made me aware of how well Manoj was doing in his acting career and they told me that he was indeed famous. Initially, I found it difficult to follow what they were saying. They told me about *India Today*, where something about *Netua* was published. I didn't know about this play before it. I haven't seen that play.'

Netua made both—Manoj Bajpayee and N.K. Sharma—stars in their circuit. Needless to say, Act One established itself from the first play.

Delhi has a rich legacy of experimental and impactful theatre. There was Shyamanand Jalan's Padatik group that staged a trilogy of Mohan Rakesh's writings such as *Rajahamsa*, *Aadhe Adhure* and *Ashadh ka Ek Din*. Then there was Girish Karnad's *Tughlaq* and Ebrahim Alkazi's *Andha Yug*. The latter had actors such as Om Shivpuri, Amrish Puri, Om Puri, Rajesh Vivek Upadhyay and Shrivallabh Vyas. The play was very well-received Then came Habib Tanvir's *Agra Bazar*, *Hirma ki Amar Kahaani* and *Charandas Chor*. Asghar Wajahat's *Jis Lahore Nai Dekhya O Jamyai Nai* started the 1990s. Actors of great calibre such as Naseeruddin Shah experimented with the writings of Manto, Premchand and Ismat Chughtai. It was indeed a great time for the Delhi theatre circuit, which saw the evolution of content, and presenters who could do justice to it.

Now, newcomers of the likes of Manoj Bajpayee, Piyush Mishra, Ashish Vidyarthi, Gajraj Rao, Vijay Raj and Anil Chaudhary were sharing the spotlight for the first time with these stalwarts of theatre.

The phenomenal success of *Netua* inspired several talented youngsters to join Act One. Nikhil Verma remembers that they did *Holi* after *Netua*. By the time *Holi* was staged, Piyush, who was the scriptwriter for this play, was back in Delhi after playing a small innings in TV and films in Mumbai. He was an NSD graduate who was in the city during 1983–86. He knew everyone, so when he joined Act One, it connected many dots. 'Manoj and I [Piyush] came really close during the musical street play *Humare Daur Mein*.'

Holi, which was a satire on the education system, was another hit presentation. Manoj played a negative role in it. You must have seen a song going viral on social media in which Piyush and Manoj are seen singing wholeheartedly on the TV show *Jeena Isi Ka Naam Hai.* This song was used in *Holi.*

Wo puraane din, aashiqaane din
Os ki nami me bheege wo suhaane din
Wo guzar gaye, hum thehar gaye
Piche mud ke dekha, paya kidhar gaye
Akele hain khade, kadam nahi badhe
Chal padenge jab bhi koi raah chal pade
Jaayenge kahan, hai kuch pata nahi
Keh rahe hain wo ki unki kuch khata nahi . . .

Barry's TAG and Act One also collaborated for *Suno Re Kissa.* Manoj, Rituraj and Ashish were in the lead roles. Divya Seth and Varsha Agnihotri also had roles in this play. Piyush had adapted the musical *Blood Brothers* into Hindi, and he was also the narrator of the show. Barry had done the casting and direction. Manoj and Rituraj played twins who were unaware of that truth. They fall for the same girl in the story. Rajiv Gaur, Manoj's friend and Barry's student, explains how the story is about a rich boy living near a slum. He is friends with a poor boy, and his mother has an issue with this. Manoj played the poor boy, while Rituraj essayed the role of the rich boy. Ashish played Rituraj's elder brother. While Divya Seth enacted Rituraj's mother, Poornima played Manoj's mother.

One unique thing was that Manoj and Rituraj played seven-, twelve-, seventeen- and twenty-two-year-olds in the same play. 'It was extremely challenging. We worked a lot on our voice and body language. Barry had faith in us and that helped us greatly,' Rituraj recalls.

The first show took place in Delhi's Shri Ram Centre. Ashok Purang recalls the show as being glorious. It had fantastic songs—typical Hollywood-style grand story. Ashok watched consecutive shows of it.

Suno Re Kissa was later telecast on Doordarshan, but not in the way Barry wanted. For some unknown reason, the channel edited it like a TV serial, which kind of took away all its fun.

By that time, Manoj was neck-deep in his theatre assignments. During this time, he wrote a letter to his father. He revealed this on Anupam Kher's show *Kuch Bhi Ho Sakta Hai*. 'I wrote Babuji a letter. I said I never told you this in my childhood, but I never wanted to be a doctor. My apologies for this. I wanted to be an actor and I have started my journey.'

His father's reply came as a pleasant surprise: 'Dear son Manoj, you have told me about your dream. But I am your father. How did you even think I didn't know you wanted to be an actor? I very well knew it.'

Another popular play from Act One's repertoire was *Jab Shahar Humara Sota Hai*. A young theatre artist Divya (name changed), who became a part of the troupe just a few days before this play, was later married to Manoj. Manoj was in the central role and as usual working hard on his character. N.K Sharma recalls it as being the most ambitious play of his career. 'Rehearsals were complete. But he [Manoj] suffered a slipped disc some five days ahead of the show. Despite this, he was adamant on doing it. We consulted all the good doctors in Delhi and they all advised him a month's rest. We didn't want to take such a risk and so decided to go ahead without him. Of course, Manoj being Manoj, he came to watch the show. We made him sit at the ticket window. Once the show started, he was sent backstage, from where he contributed as much as he could.'

Recalling this incident Manoj says: 'I had rehearsed for almost fourteen hours a day, with sometimes only four hours of sleep. I was receiving much praise, but then suddenly the injury happened. In fact, it was such a serious injury that I am struggling with backache even today owing to that. This injury is from a play titled *Uljhan*, in which I was to walk on all fours. All the muscles in my back were swollen. I did the show's rehearsals after taking injections. I cried after watching *Jab Shahar Humara Sota Hai*.'

Gajraj Rao later replaced Manoj in the play.

'We did another play called *Chauboli*,' says Rajiv Gaur. 'Manoj couldn't be a part of that because he was on bed rest. Then we did *Mahakund ka Mahadan*, which was adapted by Piyush Mishra in Hindi from an American play. Manoj was in a negative role in this one.'

During this time, Act One received an invitation to stage three plays, including *Netua*, at a theatre festival in Kolkata, and Manoj was back to grinding himself for the role.

Around the same time, Tigmanshu made him meet film-maker Shekhar Kapur, who was in Delhi for the casting of *Bandit Queen*. It was a fruitful meeting where Shekhar shortlisted him in the probables for the role of Vikram Mallah.

The core value of Act One was a unique sense of democracy. If a member wanted to work with some other group, they wouldn't be stopped from doing so. Manoj did a play titled *Court Martial* with another group. While he was seen as Major Puri, Gajraj played a defence lawyer. 'I [Gajraj] saw Manoj totally engrossed in Major Puri's character. Ranjit Bhai had directed it. Many a time, I saw Manoj acting on stage and got swept off. It was amazing how he created magic out of small moments.'

While being with Act One, Manoj worked with the Sakshi Group for *Uljhan*. It can be considered one of the top five performances of Manoj's theatre career. Saurabh Shukla adapted a Vijaydan Detha story, and it was directed by Avtar Sahni. The first show of this play, which was organized by the Sangeet Natak Akademi to inspire young directors, took place in Lucknow. 'My hand was operated on just a week before the first show,' recalls Avtar. 'There was another accident that happened during the show. Manoj, who was playing an ape-man, collided with Alka Amin, who was playing Banjari. The collision was such that they both were unconscious for close to thirty seconds. When the show finished, there was a silence of five minutes, but then the audience gave a standing ovation for five minutes.' Manoj played a character who had grown up among wolves. 'I had prepared a special jute costume for Manoj. He was so involved with the character that he started living in the costume at home.'

Manoj's friend Anil Chaudhary had also played a role in *Uljhan*. 'I played a barber in the play, but his role was quite challenging,' he confesses. 'Manoj had to walk on all fours, and then jump from one spot to another, but people still remember the dedication and sincerity with which he practised for the part. Nawazuddin Siddiqui played a tree in the play.'

Before *Uljhan*, Manoj had worked on another play titled *Maharathi* with the Sakshi Group. It was directed by Krishnakant.

Act One had written new success scripts during the Kolkata theatre festival. Then they did *Mahakund ka Mahadan*, but it didn't get a favourable response initially. Piyush Mishra takes the blame for it. 'I couldn't come up with a strong script. Though when we did the play again after a year of reworking the script, everything went fine.'

When *Mahakund ka Mahadan* wrapped up, Manoj was ready for Mumbai. Ashish Vidyarthi was already in the film industry by then. Anubhav Sinha had also started working in Bollywood.

Act One was also ready with its second generation. N.K. Sharma was an established director by then and Piyush Mishra was already famous.

Chapter 9

Darling Delhi: A Failed Affair

'I have been through a bad marriage. I fell in love with Divya [name changed], a friend from theatre. She lived in Lajpat Nagar and was from a well-to-do family. Our courtship days were golden.'

You must have heard the phrase *'Dilli dil walon ki'*, which literally means Delhi is a city of big-hearted people. So, it's impossible for a young person to not fall in love, especially when that young person is involved in the creative arts.

During his initial years in Delhi, Manoj was too preoccupied with his work and career to be distracted by anything else. 'I was shy and introverted. I could never be myself with my sisters-in-law or women in general. I was very self-conscious. This nature of mine kept me from dating in college as well because I could never initiate a conversation.'

Love never knocks before arriving though! Once he was in Nainital for three months for an acting workshop, where Parveena (name changed) was also with him. She was an informed, English-speaking girl who gave Manoj hope of finding love. He was in Delhi for more than six years by then. They spent a lot of time together. Just when he started dreaming of a life together with Parveena, one day his world came crashing down. The two of them were taking a stroll near Mandi House. A car suddenly stopped on the other side of the road and Parveena went running towards her 'friend', totally ignoring Manoj's presence. He was hurt. It was a rude shock. This incident left him heartbroken.

He had fallen in love earlier, in Class 12, which was perhaps more of a 'crush'. Whenever he heard the rhythmic 'present, sir' by Roll number 44 during the roll call, he couldn't help smiling. In fact, he would blush. His friends started teasing him as *forty-forwa*. The girl was, of course, totally unaware of these developments. Proposing to a girl in a small town was probably more difficult than climbing Mount Everest.

Manoj's friend, Anish Ranjan, remembers these times fondly. 'We devised a way to propose to the girl. Manoj had a nephew who studied at that school. For a few days, Manoj's friends tried to establish this fact by passing remarks in front of the girls.. Then one day, the nephew reached the girl and called her 'aunty' (since Manoj was his uncle). Today, you might find it all amusing, but in those days, finding out a girl's name was a challenge in itself. There was no social media, so one had to painstakingly devise other, less-obvious, ways of digging out a girl's name, without letting her know.'

Manoj wanted to go for logical progression, which was aptly supported by his friends. 'I wasn't at the spot, but I was told that he managed to confess his love for the girl in the college field. His friends were excited, but all Manoj got for an answer was: "Later",' says Rajkumar Singh. Though nobody really knows what happened "later".

After Parveena's shocking exit from their one-sided love, Manoj became a bit more sceptical about such relationships. After nearly two years, he started developing feelings for someone. By that time, he was a rising star in the Delhi theatre circuit, following the success of *Netua*. He was working with established directors such as Robin Das and Avtar Sahni. Act One was doing well for itself. Manoj was given the responsibility of conducting workshops, and this presented itself as an opportunity to meet charming women. Actor Sakshi Tanwar, who was also a part of one such workshop, shares this nugget. 'I was a member of the dramatic society in college. A Hindi play was being organized in our college and Manoj sir came to teach us. His play *Netua* was already a hit. We learnt a lot in his workshop. Our play was called *Madam* and by chance I had a nice role in it. In a way, he was my first director.'

Manoj narrated a story from that time. 'I was expected to train and perform in plays with the girls of Lady Shri Ram College, but they were very mischievous. They figured out that I was shy around women. Every time I reached college, they would whistle or say something to make me awkward. I requested the college president to send somebody to fetch me up from the gate but to no avail. One day, when I went to the washroom during recess, I heard a few girls speaking, so I remained inside for one hour! Later, they started searching for me and the girl who had shown me the way to the washroom came calling. She sent the girls outside and then asked me to come out. I can't tell you how I felt that day.'

A new girl called Divya [name changed] joined Act One. She was attracted to Manoj's grit and determination. He was getting better and better at his craft. He too liked Divya's personality, her beautiful voice and her seriousness about her work. They soon became emotionally attached. They started talking about their work and everything around it. It was a sincere attempt by them to add colour to life.

They decided to get married. 'When Manoj confided in us about his plans to get married to Divya, we suggested he talk to his parents,' says Manoj's old room-mate Nikhil Verma. 'Similarly, Divya was advised to talk to her parents. She said her parents wouldn't agree to the match. This got Manoj really worried.'

Act One was called to Kolkata for the Nandikar's National Theatre Festival. This event, which was started in 1984, took place during 16–25 December every year. It was fast gaining prominence. There was a certain tension in the air in 1992 because of the Ram Janmabhoomi agitation. Incidentally, Manoj and his team got reservations for 6 December. Girls were not allowed to be on the trip due to the sensitive environment. So, Divya didn't go either.

By the time the train reached Kanpur, Babri Masjid was demolished. The Kanpur station was filled by the chants of 'Jai Shri Ram'. N.K. Sharma, Nikhil and Manoj were in a dilemma about the future course of action. On the one hand was the promise they had made to the organizers, and on the other the fear of the situation getting worse. They finally decided to continue on their journey. The train reached Kolkata in the shadow of fear, but they were safely escorted to a guest house. The festival was cancelled eventually. After being locked up for two days in the guest house, they were made to sit in the returning train under police protection. It was an almost empty train.

Manoj too was starting to get worried about his relationship with Divya. He was not ready for marriage because it demanded a structured lifestyle, but he had already committed and there was no going back for him. Anish Ranjan shares an interesting anecdote from that time. 'I had a Priya scooter. Manoj came to my house in Siddharth Enclave and we had lunch together. We set out for a ride and after crossing Sarai Kale Khan, he confessed that he was in love. I had an inkling of who the girl was, yet I asked her name. When I asked him what he intended to do, he said he wanted to wait for six months before tying the knot. "Why wait for six months?" I asked him. "It will take me some time to arrange the money," he replied. I told him to get married in six days instead of waiting for another six months if he sensed any danger.'

The venue was finalized hastily. The date was fixed, and arrangements were made. Manoj couldn't muster the courage to tell his parents the manner in which he was getting married. It was an interfaith marriage. Plus his career was uncertain. Even if his parents agreed, they would have wanted the wedding to follow all the rituals of a Hindu wedding. What marriage meant for his family can be understood from his father's story. 'I got married when I was in BSc second year. The elderly spent an entire day discussing how the wedding procession would move. The preparations needed to be made. One day, the person whose Jeep I had brought from Delhi asked my father how he was planning to go. It was then decided that every baaraat member would find their own ride. So, there were around twelve horses, some ten elephants and close to thirty bullock carts. Whatever they could find, they rode. My wife's village Loria was about 30 km away. More than 1000 people joined in the procession. A Jeep was arranged for me. There was hardly anyone in the area who wasn't part of it. Even today, the villagers taunt us that we weren't there for the wedding but to crush them.'

Elephants in the procession had destroyed crops of the villagers who then went and complained to Geeta Devi's father.

On the contrary, Manoj wanted to have just a few close friends at this wedding. He did not want it to be an elaborate and expensive affair. Everything was kept under wraps to avoid any sort of dangers. The Arya Samaj Temple of East Delhi's Laxmi Nagar was the venue. Manoj's friend and senior journalist Rajesh Joshi recalls: 'I was working as a crime reporter in *Jansatta*. Manoj called up and said he was getting married, that too against the will of the girl's family. Divya's parents were well-off, while Manoj was not in a steady job. There were economic and cultural differences between the families as well. He said he was getting death threats. I talked to the local DCP, and he posted two armed cops outside the temple for a hassle-free marriage.'

Manoj's sister Poonam Dubey was a part of the wedding. 'I only bought clothes for Bhaiyya and Divya. I remember he was very tense during the temple wedding. He asked Divya many times to think it over before it was too late.'

Manoj's late mother said, 'He didn't tell us, and even if he did, we were not going to be a part of it. It was unthinkable to participate in such a marriage in those days. Manoj brought the girl to the village as well. There was sadness in our hearts, but we welcomed her with open arms. We treated her the way a *bahu* should be treated. She was beautiful and well spoken. Just like Divya Bharti.'

It's interesting how everything Manoj fought for in his plays such as equality, casteism and class, became a thing of debate in his own marriage. When Divya told her parents after the wedding, they reached Anish Ranjan's house, where the newlyweds were present. The first question Divya's mother asked was about the groom's occupation and his family background. Three days after this ruckus, Manoj took Divya to her house where her parents didn't allow her to return. She later left home and came with Manoj though.

How Manoj and Divya got separated is an unsolved puzzle in the actor's life. Apart from some close friends, nobody knows what exactly happened.

I remember reading on Wikipedia in 2010 about Manoj's marriage with Shabana Raza and how this was his second marriage. I thought somebody had edited Wikipedia and I wanted to edit it back, but then out of nowhere I decided to call him up. He confirmed the fact.

The whole love and marriage saga took place during 1991–95. *Bandit Queen* was yet to be released and the internet was not available in India then. He hardly spoke about this marriage in the last twenty years, except in an interview with the *Times of India*'s *Delhi Times* on 12 October 2002. 'I have been through a bad marriage. I fell in love with Divya (name changed), a friend from theatre. She lived in Lajpat Nagar and was from a well-to-do family. Our courtship days were golden. We got married, but it lost the plot once I shifted to Mumbai. I wanted to fulfil my dreams at the cost of being together. In the end, she took the decision, and we parted ways.'

Since it's a matter of the past, even friends avoid talking about it, but based on the information gathered, Divya was very young at the time of marriage and was doing her graduation. She was not ready for an institution like marriage. She probably wove a golden dream based on Manoj's initial success in Delhi theatre and finding a role in *Bandit Queen*, but that was never realized.

Then there were Manoj's own conflicts. All the facets of one's persona become visible when you start living under the same roof. Time also had its own scheme of things. His struggles in Mumbai also took a toll on their marriage. 'It's all buried in time,' says Poonam. 'We took his marriage in a healthy way, and he processed his divorce in the same manner.'

It wasn't easy for him to move on, and the pain took a long time to subside. It's not just love which fails, marriages do too.

Chapter 10

Darling Delhi: The Family Man

'Saroj bhaiyya bought a new scooter in 1993. Manoj bhaiyya used to come to Delhi from Mumbai and walk anxiously on the terrace if Saroj bhaiyya got late. He would say, "Saroj must have collided his scooter somewhere".'

During his struggling days in Delhi, Manoj's first and foremost passion was acting. But he was also aware of his family responsibilities. Though he was not obligated to send money home as the first-born, he was aware of the expectations everyone had from him.

He called his younger brother Saroj to Delhi in 1990. He had completed his graduation while living with their uncle in Bhagalpur and was now involved in farming in Belwa. Saroj had started to mould himself as per the social norms of Bihar of those days. There was much extortion and he too became a little aggressive to deal with the current scenario. And that was a cause of concern for his parents. 'I would usually return home around midnight,' Saroj recalls. 'Father was quite stressed because of my lifestyle and he wrote to Manoj bhaiyya asking him to take me out of the village. So, it was finally decided that I would move in with Bhaiyya in Delhi and take up a computer course.'

Saroj studied computers for two years. Initially, they lived separately. There was the scarcity of money as well. 'I was bored in Delhi and Manoj Bhaiyya didn't want me to return at any cost, so

64

I blackmailed him. I threatened him if we didn't have a TV by the time of the World Cup football, I would return to the village. He somehow managed the money to buy a TV.'

Manoj knew what was best for the younger brother and he didn't want Saroj to lose sight of his goal and so he kept a close eye on him. Saroj started working as an accountant after he completed the course, which paid him Rs 1200 a month. From then on, he had a steady source of income.

Once Saroj appeared to be settling down, Manoj brought his sister Poonam also to Delhi in 1992. It wasn't easy. Poonam wrote Manoj a letter describing her ambitions in life and how marriage would put an end to everything. Then Manoj somehow convinced his parents to let Poonam come to Delhi. When Manoj told his mother about his plans for his sister, she was furious. It took a lot to pacify her. When their mother broached the topic of marriage, Manoj requested them to wait for two years, till she could establish herself.

Poonam finally reached Delhi. 'The first time I arrived in Delhi, Manoj bhaiyya and his friend Yogesh Khurana brought me chhole-kulche. They told me it's Delhi's street food. Cheap and very tasty. I haven't tasted anything like that till date.'

Poonam was good at sketching, and she completed a course in fashion designing on Manoj's insistence. By this time he was already with Act One and also working with Barry. However, what he was earning wasn't enough. Despite the challenges, he fulfilled his responsibilities as an elder brother.

Poonam narrates an interesting story from those times. 'Saroj bhaiyya bought a new scooter in 1993. Manoj bhaiyya used to come to Delhi from Mumbai and walk anxiously on the terrace if Saroj bhaiyya got late. He would say, "Saroj must have collided the scooter somewhere".'

Those were trying times for Manoj, but he never backed down. His marriage was crumbling apart and his career path too was uncertain. Anybody could have disintegrated, but not him.

When Poonam started working with an export house, she once had an argument with the owner. She wanted to call it quits, but Manoj asked her to stay on. He told her to work harder and make herself a valuable resource for the company, so no one could let go of her, which was what happened eventually. Poonam ended up starting her own export house with Manoj's blessings. She is a successful fashion designer now.

Manoj's youngest sister Garima recalls: 'I was only four when he moved to Delhi. He always taught us the value of self-reliance. He made us believe in ourselves and the need for financial freedom.' Garima is a textile designer and runs a printing business in Noida.

Manoj's youngest brother, Sujeet, is an IAS officer, and he too has always been inspired by the actor.

'Whenever I went to Manoj's house, all the boys living there were so courteous and respectful that it filled my heart with joy. They always touched my feet. Later, I realized it was more out of a respect for Manoj than me,' Gajraj Rao recalls fondly.

Manoj was always a 'family man', much before the hit web series in 2019. When he was conferred with the Padma Shri in 2019, he came with his father to receive the honour at the Rashtrapati Bhavan.

Chapter 11

Darling Delhi: How I Became a Dacoit

'When I was selected for the role of Vikram Mallah, my only concern was that Nirmal Pandey shouldn't meet Shekhar Kapur, otherwise he will be picked for the character. He was so good looking. Eventually, what I feared came true.'

Through plays like *Netua, Holi* and *Suno Re Kissa*, Manoj had already become a big thing in the Delhi theatre circuit, and he was so engrossed in his theatre work that films were never a priority. Then in one evening of 1992, Tigmanshu Dhulia informed him about a possible meeting with Shekhar Kapur. Manoj wrote in his BBC article, 'I made some friends outside the boundaries of the National School of Drama. That partnership instilled theatre in my veins. I was neck-deep in theatre. The thought of moving to Mumbai and acting in films was lost somewhere in the subconscious. One day, when I was sipping tea at a road-side shop after rehearsing around ITO, I saw Tigmanshu Dhulia approaching on his old Lambretta scooter. We had tea together. He told me Shekhar Kapur wanted to meet me. I thought he was joking. Such jokes of getting a call from Spielberg and Mani Rathnam were common among us. But he was serious. He said Britain's Channel 4 was making a film on Phoolan Devi and he was the assistant and casting director, and that Shekhar Kapur had liked my photos. He insisted I meet Shekhar, and next day I went to meet him. Shekhar has this habit of speaking slowly. He eats half of the words. I had learnt English while working with Barry John. He was evaluating me for the role of Vikram Mallah, I figured this much out. Before leaving, he said I wasn't final, and he is meeting with one or two more prospects. Whatsoever happens, he would let me know.'[22]

Shekhar didn't inform Manoj and the actor kept carrying on with his theatre projects. Then he got to know that former NSD student Nirmal Pandey was meeting Shekhar for the same role for which Manoj was approached and that worried Manoj. He had a feeling he would be losing out to Nirmal. (When Nirmal Pandey passed away in 2010, Manoj wrote in his blog. 'I still remember one of his plays titled *Round Head, Peak Head*. He was exceptional in it.')

'When I was selected for the role of Vikram Mallah, my only concern was that Nirmal Pandey shouldn't meet Shekhar Kapur, otherwise he will be picked for the character. He was so good looking. Eventually it happened.'

Nirmal, who hailed from the picturesque Nainital, was very good looking and Shekhar believed it had a chain reaction on people around him. 'Nirmal was so popular among women that his attraction had a chain reaction. I had to let go of a member of the British make-up team because her love for Nirmal had started crossing boundaries.'

In Vikram Mallah, Shekhar was looking for an actor with both masculine and feminine qualities and that search ended with Nirmal. Manoj was left empty-handed.

In between, Manoj travelled to Kolkata for a theatre festival with the Act One group where he was supposed to present *Netua*, *Holi* and *Jab Shahar Hamara Sota Hai*. Upon his return, he did a few shows of *Mahakund ka Mahadan* and went to his village for a retreat. After a couple of days, he received a sensational telegram from Raghubir Yadav. Manoj's father told me, 'It was from Raghubir Yadav. We were scared for a moment after looking at it as it read "Manoj, come soon, time is waiting for you". When

I showed it to Manoj, he asked me to arrange some money as he started preparing for his return. I arranged the money—Rs 5000. Later, we got to know Shekhar Kapur had to finish *Bandit Queen* by March 1993. He had no time. He went to Naseeruddin Shah for the role of dacoit Maan Singh, but he refused, citing date issues. Eventually Manoj got the part. Manoj met the director and signed the contract for Rs 80,000.'

Like all other times, Manoj got busy with getting under the skin of the character. He started growing a beard the moment he knew the role was confirmed. He stopped brushing his teeth as well. He wanted to embrace the character, become one with it. The shooting was to commence at Dhaulpur in the beginning of 1993. All major actors, including Seema Biswas, Nirmal Pandey and Manoj Bajpayee, were called to Dhaulpur fifteen days in advance. It was the first film shooting of Manoj's life.

The behind-the-scenes chronicles of *Bandit Queen* deserves a separate book as Shekhar was making a realistic film on a character whose life was full of pain and atrocities, and that person was alive—the infamous dacoit Phoolan Devi. To avoid extreme method acting, the director would describe the scenes to the actors but didn't really give them dialogues. The actors were also taken on a trip to the dense ravines of Chambal so that they could understand the milieu.

Manoj's turn to face the camera came after a few days. 'My first scene was with Seema Biswas. I stop her from drinking from the well as I believed it was poisoned.'

A theatre veteran of ten years, Manoj got nervous in front of the camera. 'I was very nervous. I went up to Shekhar and asked if this was a long shot or a close-up? He said mid-shot. Manoj asked him how to perform in the mid-shot. He said in the same way one performs in theatre. I insisted since it's a mid-shot, I must do something differently. He asked me to mind my business and said I was paid for acting, not for the camera work!'

Since most of the characters were from a theatre background, there was a sense of camaraderie among the unit, and it also eased performance anxiety. The three months of shooting in Chambal was more like a party.

'Those were the days,' Raghubir Yadav recalls emotionally. 'We roamed around like dacoits during the day and had food together in the night. This was always followed by singing and dancing. We had taken some utensils from the police party.'

Manoj was playing the surrendered but infamous dacoit Maan Singh, and Shekhar Kapur had called Singh to the sets for Manoj's convenience. The actor was asked to observe the former dacoit's mannerism. He was staying with Manoj, but the actor was instructed not to reveal Singh's identity. 'He got clicked with everyone and distributed visiting cards. "Jai Maa Bhawani" was written on top of it. Then his name Maan Singh Yadav and "former dacoit king" in place of his designation. Whenever anybody read the whole card, their breathing would get uneasy. Maan Singh Yadav became a good friend. Whenever we went out for a little safari after shooting, he instructed the driver to move slowly at certain places and faster at others. I used to sit with him in the back. He remained cautious all the time and he had all the minute information regarding the area.'

When I tried to talk to Maan Singh, I found his new visiting card with 'former dacoit king' written in bold letters right in the middle of the card. Which means his identity never crossed beyond being a surrendered dacoit even after nearly three decades. He has played himself in a B-grade film titled *Beehad*.

There was another dacoit by the name of Maan Singh in the Chambal area before Independence, but he had a Robinhood-esque image. He was killed in an encounter in 1954. A film was made on him in 1971 with Dara Singh in the lead.

Shekhar was already a celebrated director after *Masoom* and *Mr India*, but this was new for him as well. Despite schedule pressure from Channel 4, he mostly shot in a jovial mood. Shekhar said in an *India Today* report dated 15 April 1993, 'This is the reason some of us die younger. It doesn't matter how I am feeling inside, I must look calm and composed so that the actors remain in a good mood.'

Bandit Queen received immense praise at the 1994 Cannes Film Festival. *The Economist* wrote, '*Bandit Queen* is going to change the Indian cinema forever.'[23]

The film won several accolades at various film festivals and became a hit in many countries upon screening in 1994. However, it couldn't be released in India before 25 January 1996. A person named Om Paal Singh Hoon filed a petition in the Delhi High Court two days after the film's release and its screening got halted. Its release was cleared only after a Supreme Court decision on 1 May 1996.

Bandit Queen fetched Seema Biswas, Nirmal Pandey and Saurabh Shukla much recognition, but Manoj was still not lucky. The lack of dialogues could have been a reason behind it. He had shifted to Mumbai by then. Shekhar was also a reason behind this move. Shekhar told Manoj: 'I see you guys are doing theatre for ten to twelve years. You're energetic as of now and don't care about the future. There is a kind of indifference in you towards the future and prosperity, but I don't think you're getting the right return for your talent. Are you moving forward on a goalless path? I suggest you come to Mumbai after this film. Do what you want, but at the right cost.'

Manoj said this thought process frightened him. It was like a speed-breaker that deflected a possible accident. Another complex struggle period was waiting for Manoj in the film industry.

Chapter 12

The Never-Ending Struggles of Mumbai

'It felt like I was at the wrong place. Many a time, I decided to pack my bags but kept delaying my return. Sometimes on a friend's advice, sometimes on a director's assurance. Even when I returned to Delhi for a couple of times, my friends and family members sent me back forcefully.'

After the commencement of the shooting for *Bandit Queen*, Manoj and Saurabh Shukla made Mumbai their operational ground, but that was easier said than done. Before Manoj could reach Mumbai, Mumbai came calling for him. One day, his landlord's landline phone rang and Anubhav Sinha was on the line. Anubhav had assisted Manoj in play called *Danga-83*. Anubhav asked him to quickly come to Mumbai and that he had arranged for the flight tickets.

Anubhav was assisting renowned director Pankaj Parashar then. He was making a TV serial called *Ab Aayega Maza*. He had also made a film of the same name with Farooq Sheikh and Anita Raj in the lead. He wanted a terrific actor for the serial. Parashar recalled during the show *Jeena Isi Ka Naam Hai*: 'I asked Anubhav for an actor and he said there is one of Naseeruddin Shah's calibre. I asked him to immediately call the actor.'

'Manoj arrived at my house by night. I was perplexed looking at him. He was called for the role of the hero but he was not looking like one. I took him to a spa that night only. Got him a haircut and a facial. I earned decent amount. Then I took Manoj to Pankaj. He took a good look at Manoj for two minutes and said okay,' says Anubhav.

Manoj might have found work, but the show turned out to be a pain for him as Pankaj did not like his acting. He was sent out of the project after the pilot episode itself. Manoj said in an interview, 'I shot for the whole day. I understood after two to three hours that Pankaj did not like my work. Still, I finished my schedule and went to Delhi to bring my luggage.'

Vineet Kumar was also a part of the show. 'Manoj became upset within just after three to four hours of shooting. He took me to the side and asked, 'What do I do? It seems everybody on the set is teaching me how to act." I asked him to focus on his work, and not on them.'

Anubhav threw some light on what happened there. 'Pankaj didn't like Manoj's acting. He categorically said that Manoj doesn't know how to act. Then, Sanjai Mishra replaced Manoj, but he too was asked to leave. The serial turned out to be a flop after four or five episodes.'

As per Anubhav, Pankaj left the show when it failed to leave a mark after the initial episodes and he directed the remaining four episodes, so in a way, this was the show that launched him as a director.

A few days prior to the shooting of *Ab Aayega Maza*, Manoj was in Mumbai for a workshop for the Salaam Baalak Trust, an Indian non-profit and non-governmental organization that provides support for street and working children in Delhi-NCR, when the atmosphere suddenly changed. He was trapped in a riot-like situation at a lodge in Jijamata Park. 'I picked up my Hero Honda upon hearing the news. I was staying in Jogeshwari at that time. I took him pillion and returned. All the roads were vacant that day. It was not to show any bravery but just to help a friend,' says Ashish Vidyarthi.

Another incident reinstated Manoj's belief in destiny. After the shooting of *Bandit Queen*, Manoj went to meet producer and director Prakash Jha on the insistence of Ashwini Chaudhary. Manoj was offered a major role in *Mrityudand* (1997). After the *Ab Aayega Maza* debacle, Manoj went to meet Jha, but it was a futile exercise. 'When I reached to meet Jha, I realized I have lost this role as well.'

Today, Manoj remembers this incident with a lot of grace, but it shook him from inside then. 'Manoj told me the incident upon returning,' Manoj's friend Anish Ranjan says. 'Prakash Jha was standing with some people near his building when Manoj reached there. He wanted to meet him in private for two minutes, but Prakash rudely said, "Should I come to Khandala to talk to you?"'

It was bound to pierce his heart. Anurag told me how Manoj was narrating the same incident to his friends when he first met Manoj in Mumbai.

I asked Prakash Jha regarding this incident, but he said, 'I don't remember, but we must have met. My office was in Adarsh Nagar, and everyone used to go there to meet me. All I can say is forgive me, brother, I made a mistake.'

Later, Manoj shared a great working relationship with Prakash and worked together in films such as *Raajneeti* (2010), *Aarakshan* (2011), *Chakravyuh* (2012) and *Satyagraha* (2013) together.

Manoj and Saurabh Shukla had rented a house in D.N. Nagar near Andheri. Saurabh came a few days after Manoj. 'It was a well-ventilated room on the second floor, but it came as a shock. There was an 8x8 room with a similar kitchen. The rent was Rs 2000. I lived in a big house in Delhi's Timarpur on Rs 1200 as rent. Compared to that, it was very costly, but Manoj said such things are commonplace in Mumbai. I had Rs 25,000. Out of it, I gave Manoj Rs 12,000, he also pooled in Rs 12,000 and we paid for the whole year,' says Saurabh.

Finding a house of one's liking (and more importantly, one that fits the budget) is indeed an achievement in Mumbai and therefore this called for a celebration. Manoj and Saurabh went shopping for their new home and bought furnishing from the

D.N. Nagar market. Saurabh shares an interesting incident from this time. 'While roaming around the market, we found a signboard outside a restaurant that read "Tandoori chicken Rs 12". The same item would cost Rs 35–40 in Delhi, so we decided to go for a party. Manoj asked me to place the order for the chicken. I got one plate of tandoori chicken packed. We were famished and couldn't wait to get back and have the food. But on opening the packet, we got the shock of our lives. It was hardly a 4–5-inch chicken. That was quite a rude awakening for the both of us.'

Manoj is quite fond of non-vegetarian food. During the release of *Jugaad* (2009), the makers had arranged stay at a lavish hotel for Manoj in Ghaziabad. Initially, he was very happy as it was close to his sister's house, but all his happiness vanished when he found out that the hotel didn't serve non-veg food. Delhi's well-known publicist Shailesh Giri narrates, 'We were scheduled to reach the *Hindustan Times*'s office in the morning, but Manoj said he wanted to eat non-vegetarian food first then only he would sit for interview. Interestingly, I only had Rs 1,000-2,000, while Manoj didn't keep the wallet. We had to wait for the producers to arrange the non-vegetarian food.'

The initial months in Mumbai weren't easy for Manoj. All he did was call directors and send his photographs and portfolio, only to be rejected later. There was a day when he had to face rejection from three places! 'Everything was going wrong for me. The concept of a casting director wasn't there at that time. Actors usually visited the sets to befriend the assistant directors in the hope of being offered a role. I managed to grab a role in a serial in the process. On the first day of the shooting, I gave my first shot and everyone standing in front of the camera vanished. The shot was fine from my perspective, but nobody was there to say anything. I was alone in the room. A little while later, an assistant director came in and asked me to go and change because "Madam" didn't like my work. When I reached the changing room, the costume in-charge tried to console me by saying that something similar had happened to Amitabh Bachchan, and that I shouldn't take it to heart. I simply picked up my bag and left the studio. This incident really shook me; it was bizarre and unprofessional to turn down an actor after the very first shot. To take my mind off this incident, I went to another studio where I had to shoot for a docudrama [or documentary drama] after two days, but I soon got to know that I had been replaced. Nobody cared to inform me about the shoot that was scheduled for two days later. I went back to my room, gathered some loose change and dashed to the PCO, calling the guy who had promised me a role in the serial. I was told that I did not meet the physical requirements of the lead, since they needed a taller actor. He promised me another role very soon. This way, I lost on three accounts in the same day.'

Manoj was facing rejections on every front—his height, weight, lack of sex appeal and charisma. 'There were no takers for my theatre experience. I was amazed how producers-directors didn't differentiate between a debutant or new actor and an experienced one.'

Manoj was living a life of harsh realities. The shortage of money made it harder. On top of it, there was harassment in the name of the Marathi–North Indian divide. Manoj was living in D.N. Nagar, while Vineet was staying in Juhu Scheme. One morning, Vineet found Manoj at his place, all perplexed. Apparently, Sena people were harassing him for some fundraising. Manoj had offered them Rs 5, but they were demanding Rs 101, since he was an actor!

Vineet was senior in age and experience, and he had also dealt in politics. 'I took Manoj on the bike and went straight to the local party office. I made him stand outside and asked for the local branch chief in a loud voice. This gesture made the people standing there take us seriously. Finally, a person came and accepted his fault. The matter was eventually resolved.'

Because *Bandit Queen* hadn't released in India at that time, not many knew of Manoj as an actor. 'Right after brushing my teeth, I would start thinking of how to manage breakfast, well, it mostly went unmanaged. If I could find a spot boy or a production person on any set, they would offer me food. Ashok Mehta was a top camera person. He was with us on the sets of *Bandit Queen*, so I visited him too. He knew I was hungry and always gave me something to eat. Many a time, I walked to Goregaon as I didn't have enough money for the commute.'

Meanwhile, Vijay Krishna Acharya (director of *Dhoom 3*) and Jeetendra Shastri also joined Manoj and Saurabh at their rented flat. They were all somehow managing, but none of them were getting a big break. The small roles were not of much help.

Director and cinematographer Govind Nihalani spotted Manoj and Vineet in *Ab Aayega Maza* and cast them in *Droh Kaal* (1994). Vineet got a major role in the film, which established him as an actor, but Manoj could manage just a small role. The only solace Manoj found with *Droh Kaal* was that he shared the frame with two of his favourites: Naseeruddin Shah and Om Puri. 'We talked about only two people within our theatre circle—Naseeruddin Shah and Om Puri. They might not have any reference points for their acting galore, but we learnt acting by simply watching them. They were the De Niro and Al Pacino we needed.'

Around this time, Manoj signed two serials: *Shikast* (directed by Anubhav Sinha) and *Hum Bambai Nahi Jayenge* (directed by Tigmanshu Dhulia).

Anubhav recalls those days. 'I finished writing *Shikast* and realized there's nothing for Manoj in it. I tweaked the script and created space for a mute character. Shammi Kapoor, Ashish Vidyarthi and Vineet Kumar were also part of the show. The producer changed after a few episodes. Then I got a call about Manoj leaving the show. He was angry when I contacted him.

He said he wouldn't do the serial because the producer was giving him the payment for just one episode instead of two that Manoj wanted. The producer thought Manoj didn't have dialogues in the show, so he should be paid less. Manoj abused the producer like anything. He did the initial ten or eleven episodes and was then replaced by Ashutosh Rana.'

It was heartbreaking for Manoj when the producer didn't acknowledge his contribution. 'I expected Anubhav Sinha to fight on my behalf, which he says he did, but I was very angry with him and didn't talk to him for days.'

How the team was living on the edge is evident from the incident narrated by Saurabh Shukla. 'There was a boy in the art department of *Bandit Queen*. He lived in Four Bungalows at his pilot friend's house. It was a great house with an AC in every room. We started going to that house every other day with an excuse of a party. We deliberately delayed proceedings till late in the night to experience the comfort of the AC. It was the biggest attraction.'

Manoj's role in *Hum Bambai Nahi Jayenge* could have given a fair footing to the entire Delhi gang. This one had Irrfan Khan, Nirmal Pandey, Sanjai Mishra, Vineet Kumar, Manoj Pahwa and Brijendra Kala. It was produced by BI TV, whose functional head was Shekhar Kapur at that point. However, Shekhar left the channel in some days and the serial also collapsed.

'The last few episodes of the serial were not even telecast,' says Brijendra Kala, who wrote many episodes. 'But it provided valuable experience. The soap was based on the lives of an acting school's students in which Manoj also played a student.' In a way, Manoj and Tigmanshu never found the perfect project. Though they discussed films like *Haasil* and *Yaara*, they never materialized.

Since Manoj was married, he was struggling on both fronts—personal and professional. On one such day, Divya arrived in Mumbai. Saurabh was in the house. 'I didn't know about the problems in Manoj's marriage. We welcomed Divya when she came, she knew all of us. We had a party in the evening, but everything turned awkward after that. We had just one room and left the place early in the name of work, but there was a need of space for them, so we went to another apartment in Goregaon.'

Manoj and Divya lived in the same house for some days and then shifted to Four Bungalows. For Manoj, his expenses were mounting, but there was no income. The small roles that came his way weren't enough to manage the growing expenses. In 1995, through director Imtiaz Ali, Manoj found a role in a serial called *Imtihan*. Imtiaz was Manoj's junior in college and had been in contact since the Act One days. Unfortunately, *Imtihan* received a lukewarm response.

Before this, Manoj had worked with film-maker Hansal Mehta in a serial called *Kalakaar*. He had bagged the role via Ashish Vidyarthi's recommendation. Varsha Agnihotri, his female lead in *Netua*, was his co-star in it. Unfortunately, *Kalakaar* too fizzled out after a few episodes.

On the personal front, his marriage was falling apart, and as if that was not enough, Divya decided to return to Delhi. This broke Manoj's heart. Unable to bear seeing Manoj in such a state, Saurabh brought Manoj to his Goregaon apartment. 'When I got Manoj to my place, he was in a very bad shape. He was up the whole night, staring listlessly at the ceiling fan. It got me very worried. I sensed that there was a problem that needed to be addressed immediately. I had myself gone through depression for some time during my theatre days, so I had an inkling of its gravity. I tried to reassure him that life is indeed worth living. Those days, it was raining. I had a scooter at that time. I took him pillion and reached Film City the next day. There was a lush green jungle and hillocks lined the horizon. The clouds seemed to touch the earth. I wanted the soothing natural beauty to act as balm to his frayed nerves and to help mend his broken heart. After all, what are friends for, right?'

Manoj sheds more light on those trying times. 'I wasn't doing good healthwise too at this time. Several ailments started rearing their heads. These ailments could have been treated. All they needed was discipline, but I couldn't keep my marriage intact. Financial issues only added to the woes. I couldn't prioritize: career, marriage and existence. The actor in me was completely shattered. There was no one I could turn to for emotional support and the financial situation only made matters worse. All in all, the future seemed bleak. It felt as if I was at the wrong place at the wrong time. Nothing seemed to be going my way. Many a time, I wanted to pack my bags and leave the city but for some reason or the other kept delaying my return. Sometimes on a friend's advice, sometimes on a director's assurance. Even when I returned to Delhi for a couple of times, my friends and family members sent me back forcefully.'

Nothing seemed to be improving in Mumbai. Whenever Manoj had no money for food, he would visit a friend at dinner time or lunch time in the hope of being offered food. Manoj, in an interview, said, 'Whenever we reached Anubhav Sinha's house, he sipped expensive scotch and cheap rum was served to us.'[24]

He had said this in jest, but the media blew this statement out of proportion. When I brought this up with Anubhav, this is what he had to say: 'Manoj was into dark rum those days. I don't know what he drinks now. I might have asked him in good humour if he is worthy of having whiskey. That he should have rum instead. What's the big deal?'

The years from 1993 to 1994 were particularly tough. Manoj failed to bag substantial projects, earn enough money and, most importantly, his marriage was in a shambles. He returned to Delhi after his separation with his wife, anxious and subdued. He had hit rock bottom. Since he had married Divya without his parents' consent, he felt like he had failed them as well. Theirs was the first incident of divorce in his entire family. All of this was very hard to absorb.

Poonam talks about those difficult times and how it impacted the family as well. 'Manoj bhaiyya was in deep depression. We were so uncertain that Saroj bhaiyya and I used to hold his hand while he slept.'

Time heals everything, but sometimes the pain gets prolonged. Once again he started going to Mandi House. His old friends tried to bring back his confidence, and eventually the time came when Manoj decided to return to Mumbai. Gajraj Rao was given the task of safely seeing Manoj off to Mumbai. They travelled by Rajdhani Express and reached Vineet Kumar's place when they landed in Mumbai.

However, Manoj's fight against depression was not over. At times he would bang his head against the wall, but it was his personal battle which only he could fight and win, which he eventually did. 'During this phase of confusion, dilemma and hardships, I was offered a role in a serial called *Swabhimaan.*'

Chapter 13

Swabhimaan

'Mahesh Bhatt got up and told everyone, "This man is a very big actor." Then he told me, "Your face says that you are about to leave this city, but you shouldn't do so. This city will give you a lot."'

Director Mahesh Bhatt has played a significant role in Manoj's life. He trusted Manoj during the darkest phase of his life. They met for the first time on the sets of a Doordarshan serial *Swabhimaan*. Manoj would have lost out on this project also had it not been for Ashok Purang. When Manoj arrived for the serial's casting, he talked to Bhatt's assistant directors. 'Manoj found the role to be fine, but an artist's ego came in the way,' says Ashok. 'He let go of the offer because he was offered less money. When we stepped out, he told me what had happened. Before he could say anything more, I ran inside and requested the casting director to give us half an hour to decide. I reasoned with Manoj, and he finally took up the offer.'

He did not expect to be paid Rs 2000, since he'd been paid Rs 6000 for a pilot episode a few days ago. But adversities forced him to compromise on the money part. 'I took this as a training. I decided to explore myself in front of the camera.'

Initially, he was hired for nine or ten episodes, but he caught Bhatt's eyes in the editing room. Mahesh Bhatt shared this experience in *Jeena Isi ka Naam Hai*. 'I saw him in a scene in

Manoj Bajpayee receives the National Award for Best Actor (*Bhonsle*) from former Vice President of India M. Venkaiah Naidu in 2021

Manoj receives the Padma Shri from former President of India Ram Nath Kovind

Manoj's mother, the late Smt Geeta Devi and father, the late Shri Radhakant Bajpayee

Manoj's ancestral home in his village Belwa, West Champaran

Manoj's new home in Belwa

Manoj's school in Belwa

Father Christopher Kerketta

Manoj at K.R. Senior Secondary School with his wife Shabana Raza, daughter Ava Nayla and Father Christopher Kerketta (seated in the front row)

Kamini Shukla, Manoj's sister

Manoj with his siblings. (From left): Garima, Saroj, Poonam, Kamini and Sujit

Srinjay Bajpayee, Manoj's nephew

Manoj with his daughter Ava Nayla

Srinjay Bajpayee, Manoj's nephew

Manoj with wife Shabana Raza and daughter Ava Nayla

On the set of the film *1971*. (From left): Kumud Mishra, Amrit Sagar (director), Manoj, Salman and Ravi Kishan

Poster of the National Award-winning film *1971*

Manoj with Prakash Jha on the set of *Raajneeti*

Manoj shares a light moment with actor Sharib Hashmi

Manoj with Sharib Hashmi on the set of *The Family Man*

Manoj during his theatre
days in Delhi

Manoj in his play *Netua*

Manoj during the shoot of *Bhonsle*

Manoj with Pankaj Tripathi and Vineet Kumar

Manoj in a
pensive mood

Manoj during the
shoot of *1971*

Manoj with actor Gajraj Rao during the shoot of
Hungama Hai Kyon Barpa

Manoj with Sharib Hashmi and actor
Sunny Hinduja

Manoj in the spotlight

which he was completely drunk. It was a long scene and Manoj was doing it in one take. Manoj's style and expressions were so unique that I got mesmerized.'

Bhatt sent a pager message to Manoj, asking for a quick meeting. Despite not believing the message to be genuine completely, a docile Manoj reached Filmistaan Studio where Bhatt was shooting *Chaahat* with Shah Rukh Khan. Bhatt immediately hugged Manoj. 'A successful director embraced a desperate actor. I can't explain that experience in words. My veins started twitching. Dead muscles bulged up. Unbounded energy came to the fore,' remembers Manoj.

Manoj has talked about this incident in Anupam Kher's chat show *Kuch Bhi Ho Sakta Hai*. 'Mahesh Bhatt got up and told everyone, "This man is a very big actor." Then he told me, "Your face says that you are about to leave this city, but you shouldn't do so. This city will give you a lot."'

Praise from the acclaimed director gave Manoj hope. 'I was signed for ten episodes. Then I was told I have to shoot for a few more. I was given more dialogues on screen. When the ten episodes for which I was taken on wrapped up, I asked one of Bhatt's assistants if I was needed to come the next day. "What are you saying? You're in high demand. Keep coming till we ask you not to".'

Manoj's remuneration was also increased to Rs 2500. His stature was also increasing. He became friends with his *Swabhimaan* co-actor Harsh Chhaya, who has an interesting story to share. 'Manoj was getting married in a scene. I was also in the scene. We were all sitting. He wore a grey suit and grey tie for the sequence. Rohit Roy came from the front, and I told Manoj that Rohit was looking more like a groom than him. He got hurt. He became adamant on getting his costume changed. How come Rohit looked a better groom when it's he who is getting married? Even today when we sit with friends from our *Swabhimaan* days, they accuse me of instigating Manoj.'

Manoj worked in 250 episodes of *Swabhimaan* and carved an identity for himself in the industry. By this time, he had also started doing well financially. He didn't have to worry about his next meal. 'I started going to Holiday Inn without any fear or hesitation. Earlier, I was actually afraid of the moustached gatekeeper. Those days were behind us when we had just Rs 5 in our pocket and we would have to cut short our travel before the meter touched the expected point.'

Even Manoj's father praised him for his performance in *Swabhimaan*. 'Babuji told me over the phone how my acting reminded him of Motilal—that it was very realistic.'

Because of his proximity to Mahesh Bhatt, Manoj was able to get his daughter Pooja Bhatt's Shashtri Nagar home on rent. In the meantime, he also got a cop's role in *Dastak* (1996), Miss Universe Sushmita Sen's debut film. The film didn't work at the box office, but it took Manoj to Seychelles and also got him some money.

Manoj's friendship with Pooja turned out to be even more fruitful when he bagged Salim Khan's role in *Tamanna* (1997). This film gave Manoj a chance to showcase his acting skills in front of a stalwart like Paresh Rawal. *Tamanna* was perhaps the film that put Manoj in the spotlight and people started to take notice of his acting.

The mentor–mentee relationship between Mahesh Bhatt and Manoj Bajpayee can't be explained better than the off-camera incident that happened on the sets of *Tamanna*. 'Babuji was very sick at that time. My second sister was getting married. Although I was doing fairly well money-wise, I wasn't in a position to handle all the familial responsibilities. When Bhatt saab found out about it, he gave me a hefty sum. When I returned from my village, I got busy with the shooting of *Tamanna*. I had to deliver a long speech in one scene, which was okay-ed in one take. Bhatt saab congratulated me and said I could keep the money he had given me earlier as a token of appreciation. I knew he wouldn't take the money back, but this grand gesture made me officially free from the debt. No ordinary person could have done so.'

How important the money was can be gauged from the fact that it took care of two weddings in the family, and also a severely ill father. 'I got married on 22 April 1996,' says Poonam. 'Saroj bhaiyya got married on 20 April. Due to illness, we had brought Babuji to Ranchi, where I was getting married. Maa was not ready to delay the wedding. Manoj bhaiyya asked us to reach Ranchi and said he would somehow manage the money and then come there.'

Mahesh Bhatt and Manoj Bajpayee share an emotional bond. Bhatt saab taught Manoj to express his emotions without getting scared or without any inhibitions. Mahesh Bhatt explained to Manoj how to meet and talk to journalists and how much to share with them.

Pooja Bhatt and Manoj Bajpayee received much appreciation for their work in *Tamanna*. Alia Bhatt played a young Pooja in the film. Manoj had high expectations from *Tamanna* as it was a Mahesh Bhatt film and was supposed to have a country-wide release. In 1996, Govind Nihalani's *Sanshodhan* also released, but nobody paid any heed to it or to Manoj in it. This film was based on the law that paved way for 33 per cent reservation for women in village panchayats. Stating the ground realities, *Sanshodhan* had Manoj and Vanya Joshi in the lead roles. The film was a collaboration between the National Film Development Corporation and UNICEF. The film also featured Vineet Kumar, Lalit Parimoo and Ashutosh Rana, but a limited release stopped it from making any ripples.

Tamanna was directed by Mahesh Bhatt and produced by Pooja Bhatt. Pooja wanted to organize a premier of *Tamanna* in Patna. 'Pooja was stubborn about having a premier in Patna,' says Anish Ranjan. 'At that time, ensuring film personalities' safety in Bihar was a daunting task. We used our political connections. It was necessary to attach Lalu Prasad Yadav to the proceedings, otherwise it would have been difficult for heroines in Patna, given the state's sky-high crime rates and the constant fear of people disrupting security arrangements. When we reached Patna, Pooja was amazed to see the security arrangements. Thousands were outside the theatre. Manoj and I escorted Pooja inside the theatre, but the bouncer gatekeeper stopped Mahesh Bhatt as he didn't recognize him. The famous poet and writer Janki Ballabh Shastri was also present at the event. Chief Minister Lalu Yadav arrived with his wife Rabri Devi and their children. The atmosphere was so charged up when Lalu arrived that Pooja remarked, "He seems to be a bigger star than any of us." The CM praised Manoj and addressed Pooja as *beti*, or daughter. Later, after the event, we were invited to his residence.'

There was a press conference the next day, which turned out to be chaotic and created headlines. A young reporter asked Pooja when she was going to be Bihar's daughter-in-law. He probably wanted a provocative answer as he was match-making Manoj and Pooja. This irked Manoj to such an extent that he slapped the reporter, and everybody left the conference.[25] *Tamanna* released in 1997, but it failed to put the box office on fire. Manoj's work was appreciated by the critics, but nobody saw a typical hero in the old man's character.

Swabhimaan had already wrapped up by 1996. Manoj's expectations from the Bhatt camp had taken a hit. Manoj has written at one place, 'Though Mahesh Bhatt gave me small roles in *Tamanna* and *Dastak*, after a while the future started looking bleak. This phase hurt more than the rejection phase. I was feeing worthless. I questioned myself if I knew acting, were those accolades in the theatre false? If I am living in denial?'[26]

Manoj auditioned for a short role in Ram Gopal Varma's (fondly called Ramu) *Daud* (1997) during this transitional phase. It was his first meeting with Ramu, which was about to change his life, forever. 'Kannan Iyer, who had made *Ek Thi Daayan* (2013), was Shekhar Kapur's assistant in *Bandit Queen*. He was writing *Daud* for Ramu. He told me that Ramu was looking for Paresh Rawal's right-hand man. He had asked Irrfan Khan and Vineet to show up for auditions and wanted me to come too. I asked for the remuneration. It was Rs 35,000. I thought that would take care of a few months' rent. When I reached the set for an audition, Irrfan and Vineet were there too. When my turn came, Ramu asked me, "What have you done before?" "*Bandit Queen*," I replied. "I have seen *Bandit Queen* twice. Which role did you play?" he asked. "Maan Singh," I said. He stood up and asked me if I was being truthful. I answered in the affirmative. "But you are so young!" he said. "Sir, I had grown a beard for that role and the character was artificially aged as well." He said he had been searching for me for five years, and that nobody was able to tell him my name or give him my contact number. "Don't do this role. I have a lead role for you in my next," he said. And the rest as they say is history.'

Manoj found it surprising that Ramu was impressed by a role that nobody talked about. After all, it was a mute character. 'Everyone got busy with work after *Bandit Queen*. Saurabh Shukla was busy in serials. Seema Biswas was doing *Khamoshi: The Musical* (1996). Aditya Srivastava had also gotten a project. I was probably the only one without work. I liked what RGV had said, but I remembered it's been four years in Mumbai, and I had heard such promises many times before. I told Ramu that I wanted to do *Daud*. I was offered Rs 35,000. "I will make a film with you after *Daud*," he promised.'

There are many implications of the short story of Ramu and Manoj's first meeting. First, one shouldn't give up putting in an effort. You never know who arrives to guide you towards your destination. Second, it's hard to get anything before the right time and before fate wills it. Third, directors become big because of their ability to spot talents, and not because they have made some hit films.

First it was Mahesh Bhatt and then Ram Gopal Varma who put a price on Manoj's talent. RGV offered Manoj a role in *Daud* only on his face value, but it brought Manoj to a race he always wanted to be in.

Mahesh Bhatt had said this about Manoj in *Jeena Isi Ka Naam Hai* in 2003: 'I can predict Manoj's future today. I think time has taken a turn. There are so many new directors for who Manoj is an ideal actor. Manoj is just the right fit for their enthusiasm and style. A generation of directors which believed a person with common features couldn't be a hero, is getting obsolete. I would suggest Manoj to stay at the crease and keep scoring singles if he can't hit a six. He has a great future.' Manoj took this in his stride and kept scoring runs before he became a valuable asset in all formats of the game.

Chapter 14

Satya: Mumbai ka King Kaun?

'For Bhiku's character, I took inspiration from a Bihari guy who lived in my home town. He was a Jeetendra fan and wore printed shirts like him. I imbibed his temperamental behaviour.'

'Mumbai ka king kaun?' [Who is the king of Mumbai?] If Manoj Bajpayee hadn't done any other film in his career, he still would have been recognized in Hindi film history because of this one dialogue in *Satya* (1998). Such was the popularity of this dialogue! However, it wasn't a part of the script and was improvised by Manoj during the scene.

Satya is much more than a film. Apart from having a cult following even after two decades, it gave birth to many stars who would rule the Hindi movie industry in the coming years. It gave hope to millions who were facing rejections. It changed the rules and results of the game forever. It put a stop to formula films for a while and pushed young film-makers to go for what they wanted. It created history, to say the least.

What Ramu promised Manoj during the casting of *Daud* wasn't false. Ramu knew what he was capable of! Anurag Kashyap recalls: 'I still remember Manoj's first scene in *Daud*. In this scene, Paresh Rawal was freaking out when Manoj enters behind him with a gun in his hand. Ramu was very impressed with Manoj's work, his expressions in this scene. He took Manoj aside after the scene and said he wanted to make a different film with him.'

Ram Gopal Varma had been planning to make a film on the Mumbai underworld since *Daud*. He said in an interview, 'I was making *Daud* with Sanjay Dutt after *Rangeela* [1995]. He knew a lot about the underworld due to his own issues, and he shared them with me. I had James Hadley Chase's novel *My Laugh Comes Last* in mind. Truth be told, I made a film titled *Antham* in Telugu in 1992, which was released in Hindi as *Drohi* [1992]. It flopped. I understood my mistakes and turned the original story into *Satya*. Urmila was in the previous film as well.'[27]

This meant *Satya* wasn't an original story, but its treatment was new and realistic. Ramu shared his idea with Manoj during the shooting of *Daud* and gave him the responsibility of making him meet the new talents from the theatre world. Interestingly, Manoj might have been finalized for the film, but the project still lacked the basics like a title and a script. It was 1996. 'Ramu needed someone to elaborately write his idea. I knew Vinod Ranganathan and arranged for a meeting. Vinod had written *Satya*'s script, but his draft didn't impress Ramu.'

Vinod was one of the writers of *Swabhimaan* and was friends with Manoj. Then Manoj took a 'gem' to Ramu—Anurag Kashyap. Manoj and Anurag shared an emotional bond. 'Anurag met Ramu with high energy. Ramu was impressed. Their collaboration worked,' says Manoj.

Then Saurabh Shukla also joined the team as a writer since Ramu couldn't trust Anurag completely as he was very young at the time. 'When names might have been proposed to Ramu, both Manoj and Anurag would have taken my name for sure,' says Saurabh Shukla. 'Anurag knew my work. I didn't know him much though. I wanted to stay away from writing. Then Ramu gave me a deal. He offered me the role of Kallu Mama along with the writer.'

Initially, Ramu had offered Manoj the central role of Satya but changed it to Bhiku Mhatre once the script began to take shape.

The central role was given to Southern actor J.D. Chakravarthy, who had worked with Ramu in *Shiva* (1989). It jolted Manoj. After *Bandit Queen*, he was again not given the central role. He had to accept the role despite overflowing emotions. 'Manoj was upset on losing the role of Satya,' says Anurag Kashyap. 'We are small-town people. The film is called *Satya* and somebody else is doing that role, it is bound to feel bad. Sometimes, I would receive Manoj's call in the morning where he would say that everything had gone haywire. The heroine is also not there with me any more. We kept convincing him during the shoot about how the character of Bhiku is taking great shape and that everything was fine. After all, we were the ones writing the film.'

To see the positives in it, Manoj was destined to play Bhiku. The backdrop of finding names for both the lead characters in the film is also very interesting. When Saurabh and Anurag were banging their heads over the possible names of the characters, they heard Ramu calling 'Bhiku, three coffee.' This was how they decided on Manoj's name in the film. The Marathi surname 'Mhatre' was added by Manoj later. Ramu explained the nomenclature of Satya, 'There are two reasons of *Satya* being the film's title. It was a tribute to Govind Nihalani's *Ardh Satya*. Second, my first girlfriend's name was *Satya*. Truth be told, she wasn't my girlfriend, I loved her, but she never knew I existed. With this name, I wanted to convey to her how I have fared in life.'

Anurag Kashyap, Saurabh Shukla, Manoj Bajpayee and Ram Gopal Varma formed a team that was cynical and experimental. The post-production of *Daud* and pre-production of *Satya* were going on simultaneously. Most of the meetings took place at Ramu's house in Four Bungalows. In one such meeting, Manoj met a young Apurva Asrani. He was a nineteen-year-old kid in Ramu's team who later edited *Satya*. Manoj and Apurva hit it off and they would roam around in Apurva's old Kinetic Honda. Apurva wrote on his blog, 'Sometimes Manoj shared a couple of drinks with my father. During this time, Manoj and I made a pact that whenever I will direct a film, he would take only Rs 2 as fees. This contract was written on a paper napkin, and I believe it will happen at the right time.'[28]

Apurva later wrote *Aligarh* (2015) for Hansal Mehta, which is a milestone film in Manoj's career. Though that paper napkin contract is yet to be tested!

As the script progressed, Manoj was getting deeper into the character. 'Anurag and I prepared Bhiku's backstory. I wasn't aware of the Mumbai underworld, but I had seen many criminals in Bihar. I focused on them and realized that if we leave the language part aside, the struggle for power is more or less the same. For 'Bambaiyaa Hindi', I saw a trainer in my domestic help, who was from Kolhapur. The mafias in films, before *Satya*, usually wore white clothes and smoked cigars. I gave Bhiku one black vest, two black jeans and a few printed shirts from my wardrobe that I bought from Hill Road. There were fourteen such shirts in all. I bought them all and gave a colourful outlook to the gang leader who was dark from the inside. I lived, ate and slept with this character for five months. I dreamt of Bhiku. Anurag and Ramu helped in preparation.'

The experiences of living in Bettiah also came handy. Manoj said in an interview, 'For Bhiku's character, I took inspiration from a Bihari guy who lived in my home town. He was a Jeetendra fan and wore printed shirts like him. I imbibed his temperamental behaviour.'[29]

Needless to say, the way Manoj presented Bhiku Mhatre on screen, it was destined for success. The shooting of *Satya* started in August 1997. A scene involving Sushant Singh and J.D. Chakravarthy was getting shot on the third day. This scene had Sushant Singh asking JD for extortion money and JD attacking him on the face with a knife. It was a simple scene, but when it happened, Sushant screamed in pain. Manoj Pahwa, who was standing nearby, screamed for water, but Ramu didn't say cut. The whole scene was improvised. Ramu later said Sushant's scream changed the entire film and its dynamics. Everybody was asked not to mouth already written dialogues after this point. 'The way Ramu reacted to this scene, I hadn't seen it before,' says Anurag. 'He tore the script written by Saurabh and me and threw it in the dustbin. On 12 August itself, Gulshan Kumar was murdered, and the shooting was stalled.'

The murder of Gulshan Kumar was a big event, and it induced some changes in the script as per the new equations of the underworld. *Satya* never followed a fixed script though. Scenes were written and shot, and the characters were worked upon. For example, the script didn't have any mention of Bhiku's rattling laugh. 'One day we were shooting at Ramu's Bandra house when Manoj laughed in a peculiar way,' recalls Anurag. 'It was his nervous laughter. We all liked it and made it a part of his character.'

Saurabh Shukla cites another example of improvisation. 'Bhiku gets hold of one of Gurunarayan's men in a scene. I am eating dosa on a nearby table. While it goes on, I suddenly pick up the revolver and shoot the hanging man. We were doing this scene. The moment I fired the gun, Manoj screamed, *"Bata ke maarna chahiye na, yaar, bahra karega kya?"* He inserts fingers in his ears while saying so. This wasn't in the script. It was improvised."

Anurag seconds this though. 'Throughout the shooting, Manoj and the other actors lifted the film at many points with their acting. I understood improvisation during *Satya*.'

Manoj's dance in the song 'Sapne me milti hai' was also an improvisation. It was the first song of his career where he was supposed to dance like nobody is watching. He wasn't ready for the '1-2-3' style choreography then. On top of it, the atmosphere on the sets was such that everyone wanted to do something new. 'Choreographer Ahmed Khan was worried how he would make people like Manoj and Saurabh dance! He asked Ramu for a solution. Ramu said he would see at the location. Ahmed was going mad. We reached the location. Ramu set the frame and pointed towards a spot and said, "Your wife will stand there. You will suddenly enter the scene and start dancing." Ramu said he didn't want to see Manoj Bajpayee but Bhiku Mhatre.' The dance that followed was historic. 'I couldn't even think Manoj could dance. He did steps that were not even steps,' Makarand Deshpande says.

Manoj was trained in a semi-classical dance Chhau, but in 'Sapne me milti hai', he took the wedding procession dance a step ahead. His expressions weren't governed by any dance rules.

In a scene, Manoj refused to stand on a rock. 'Anurag and I rehearsed for this scene. I had to stand on the edge of a rock at Bandstand. But I have vertigo. I finished the scene with some difficulty. I still don't understand how this one line became so iconic.'

This line was 'Mumbai ka king kaun?'

'Manoj was scared of heights, so I grabbed his legs before every take. It was funny,' says Anurag.

Manoj sometimes felt inferior in front of J.D. Chakravarthy as he believed Ramu was giving him more importance. They were both Telugu-speaking and knew each other because they had worked on *Shiva*. Actor Harsh Chhaya says, 'Manoj would sometimes complain that Ramu was giving extra weightage to Chakravarthy.'

Harsh was married to Shefali, who played Bhiku's wife in the film, then, so Manoj, Harsh and Shefali used to meet even after the shooting. Manoj was the one who took Shefali to Ramu.

He did another favour for Saurabh Shukla. Barnali Ray was assisting Ramu on *Satya*. Saurabh and Barnali became thick friends. However, when Saurabh proposed to her, she didn't reply and went home to Kolkata. Saurabh tells me, 'Barnali is ten years younger to me. She liked me as a friend but wasn't sure about marriage. I was at an age where I felt lonely. Manoj and other friends wanted me to get married. When Barnali returned, Manoj sat her down and said I was a good boy. Decent and truthful. Pure hearted. Sang too. He really convinced her. I can say he had a big hand in my marriage to her.'

Manoj and Ramu had become close friends by the last shot of *Satya*. Manoj didn't have his own car, but they roamed around in Ramu's red Maruti Esteem to studios and restaurants. Manoj also took his childhood friend Anish Ranjan to Ramu in November 1997. Anish's father had died a few days ago and Manoj wanted him to come to Mumbai. Anish's sister Kanika had already arrived in Mumbai as Hansal Mehta's assistant. She was like a sister to Manoj. 'Manoj sketched a plan via Ramu to have me stay in Mumbai, and I did,' says Anish.

He joined Ramu's company as a writer.

During the editing of *Satya*, Manoj was selected for Ramu's Telugu film *Prema Katha* (1999). This film started Antara Mali's career and later she became an integral part of the Ramu camp. With *Prema Katha* it was evident that Manoj had become a part of the Ramu camp and he didn't need to see the struggles he faced after *Bandit Queen*.

'*Satya*'s success was unimaginable. I showed the first cut to fifteen people, and all trashed it. One of my uncles advised me to not even release it if possible. And the person they hated the most was Manoj Bajpayee,' recalls Ramu. Ramu incorporated some suggestions and then started the trials. The first was in Famous Studio. 'Our minds stopped working when we watched the film. Such was its impact. We realized it's going to be Bhiku Mhatre's film even if it is named *Satya*,' says Makarand Deshpande.

Manoj met Amitabh Bachchan for the first time during this trial. It was a dream come true for Manoj. The superstar of the millennium was standing right in front of him. The man who had inspired generations of actors. Manoj was tipsy during the meeting. 'Ram Gopal Varma, Khalid Mohamed and I were drinking in a car outside the trial show theatre. Ramu left before the film's climax, but I couldn't muster the courage to meet Bachchan sir in that state. I don't know what Khalid Mohamed thought, but he asked me to come out of the car. He shut the doors from inside when I went outside. I didn't have any option other than going inside the theatre. I wanted to hide in the washroom, but the film got over before I could reach there. Abhishek saw me, and he started praising my acting. Then I felt a towering man coming from behind. Amitabh Bachchan was heaping praise on me, but it all felt like a whistle. I couldn't understand anything. In the end, I asked if I could hug him. He agreed. Of our first meeting, I only remember embracing him.'

Here was the man whose *Zanjeer* (1973) inspired Manoj to take up acting as a career. Manoj told the *Indian Express*, 'I was small when I watched *Zanjeer*. It was the first time I felt like becoming an actor. His amazingly believable acting left a deep mark on me.'[30]

Harsh Chhaya had seen a show of *Satya* with Manoj. 'I remember when we were going to watch *Satya*, we gifted Manoj a watch. It was a metaphor for how his time has arrived.'

It was indeed a prophecy!

Satya released on 3 July 1998. Manoj couldn't sleep the previous night. He was anxious about the audience acceptance. On top of everything, it was given an 'A' certificate. 'I stayed in the Shashtri Nagar area of Andheri West. I grew closer to Mahesh Bhatt during *Tamanna* and he had rented his flat to me. Anurag had also come to that flat. I was extremely anxious. I wanted to see the audiences' reaction to my work. How do they react upon seeing me? So, I kept visiting different theatres with either Anurag or somebody else and kept telling Ramu everything. Ramu, in his own way, addressed our concern about the lack of footfall in theatres. For some reasons, he was confident of the audience's love. And it happened. Crowds started flocking in after the first week. They had liked Bhiku Mhatre. I remember the main poster of the film had J.D. Chakravarthy, aka Satya, in prominence. Sometimes it was JD and Urmila Matondkar. I was nowhere, but there was a hoarding on Juhu Chaupati. I was on it with JD and Urmila. I was holding a pistol in it. That one hoarding gave me hope. Whenever I crossed Juhu, I looked at that hoarding and consoled myself. On the night of the release, Anurag and all other friends gathered under that hoarding and drank and had fun.'

To celebrate this, there was another party at Manoj's Shashtri Nagar house. At one point, the party became so wild that almost all the guests got completely drunk before proceeding to tear off each other's clothes and strip each other naked. One person present there described it as a bizarre party. But, not everyone left on a happy note. Saurabh Shukla reprimanded Manoj like no one's business.

Satya couldn't sustain itself in many small cities for even one week. 'The first week saw 20–25 per cent occupancy and it seemed like the film was not going to work. We were told that the film was taken down on the second and third day of screening in cities such as Allahabad in north India. Ramu was still composed. We understood it later. It picked up from the second week due to tremendous publicity by word of mouth. People who had watched the film were recommending it to their friends and relatives. It was getting difficult for me to walk on the road without being recognized. They would shout "Bhiku-Bhiku".'

Satya turned out to be one of the highest-grossing films of 1998. Manoj's late father told me, 'We had gone to Mumbai after a few days of *Satya*. One day we were standing at Bombay Central when people came screaming: "Bhai has come, bhai has come".'

Manoj was a star, and its success had bigger implications. Anupama Chopra wrote in *India Today* on 20 July 1998, 'Despite some loopholes, *Satya* is a milestone. This takes Bollywood films a step ahead and gives hope that one day different streams of films will co-exist.'

It was an award-winning performance. Manoj won the Best Actor (Critics) award at the Filmfare Awards of 1999. He was anonymously declared the winner by the jury. He won the Best

Supporting Actor at the Zee Cine Award. His parents were present at the event. Even before the award was announced, the crowd started chanting 'Bhiku-Bhiku'. This must have meant the world to his farmer father.

At Star Screen Awards, Manoj came with his parents. Prakash Jha was also there. Anish Ranjan was also there. Prakash Jha asked Manoj about his parents. Jha bent and touched their feet when Manoj confirmed. It was surprising because this was the same person who refused to recognize Manoj during his struggling days. It must have been an honour for Manoj's parents because Prakash Jha also hailed from Bettiah, and he had made a name for himself in the industry for many years.

This was a time when Manoj could be seen everywhere, at all award show. However, it was his mother whose advice topped all the accolades he won. 'I wanted Maa-Babuji to come to the award shows. *Satya* was making all the right noises. During one award show, my mother said in Bhojpuri, "It's good to receive awards, but don't take them as fools who haven't won awards".'

Chapter 15

Shabana

'When I arrived at the party, a girl caught my eye. She was without make-up and with oiled hair and a pair of spectacles. I told myself that no Bollywood heroine had the courage to arrive at a party with oil in her hair. Her simplicity won me over.'

Satya's success added fame and female friends to Manoj's life, but none of them seemed long term to him.

Film parties have their own purpose. Sometimes they make lovers meet, and at other times, bring talents together. It's the place where creative juices flow and take over real drinks. One such party was organized on the completion of 100 episodes of a Hansal Mehta serial. 'I returned home after shooting *Kaun*. We were doing back-to-back night shifts. I was tired and thought I wouldn't be able to attend the function. Then I received a call from Vishal Bhardwaj that he was running late, so I had to escort his wife, Rekha, to the party. I knew Vishal and Rekha from my Delhi days, so I readily agreed. When I arrived at the party, a girl caught my eye. She was without make-up and with oiled hair and a pair of spectacles. I told myself that no Bollywood heroine had the courage to arrive at a party with oil in her hair. Her simplicity won me over.'

Shabana, the girl at the party, was at that time famous as the heroine of Vidhu Vinod Chopra's big-budget film *Kareeb* (1998).

Neha, which was her name, was at that time suffering from depression. *Kareeb* didn't click at the box office, and she had no other offers in her kitty except *Hogi Pyaar ki Jeet* (1999) because of the agreement she had signed with Vidhu Vinod Chopra. She reached out to her director-friend Rajat Mukherjee. Rajat was going to Hansal's party at Sun-n-Sand and he asked Shabana to come along. When she reached there, Rajat and Anish convinced her to attend the party. Because she wasn't prepared for it, she arrived in a very non-party-like attire. She met Manoj for the first time, and sparks flew.

'Frankly, I wasn't planning to be at the party for long. Manoj was also waiting for Vishal Bhardwaj to arrive, but we both ended up staying till the end,' remembers Shabana.

After the party at Sun-n-Sand, Manoj, Shabana, Rajat, Hansal and Anish went to the discotheque at Bawa International, where they had a great time. Later, they went to Rajat's house, where the party continued till four in the morning. Shabana and Manoj hit it off instantly and they enjoyed each other's company.

'It felt nice—being with Manoj. We didn't talk much, but the closeness felt good. Something clicked. I felt a strong bond. There wasn't any reason or old story behind it. I found myself asking after a few weeks: *Is everything right with me? Is this some sort of infatuation?*'

By this time, Manoj's career had gathered momentum and Shabana was shooting for whatever films she had in her kitty. Saurabh Shukla also takes some credit for Manoj and Shabana's friendship. 'Vidhu Vinod Chopra wanted a very innocent-looking girl for *Kareeb*. I had seen Shabana during a telefilm shoot in Delhi. With her permission, I sent her photographs to Vidhu. He liked them. Then, Shabana was called for the screen test in Mumbai and that is how she landed the role in *Kareeb*,' says Saurabh.

Kareeb and *Satya* released in July 1998. One was a hit; the other a flop. Shabana's career was at stake. 'We were both living in the vicinity but at different addresses. We kept meeting. Sometimes I would stay back at Shabana's place and sometimes she would stay back at mine, especially when we had a party.'

Around the same time, Manoj and his team started planning to make a film based on the play *Netua*. Manoj and Shabana were finalized for the lead roles, but somehow it didn't materialize.

Manoj and Shabana married many years later, but they had committed to each other long ago. That's why Shabana had arranged for a meeting between Manoj and her family. Manoj had also started giving signals to his family. When Manoj's sister Poonam became a mother, Shabana came with a gift on behalf of Manoj. Shabana also visited Belwa village on the occasion of the wedding of Manoj's youngest sister, Garima, which took place on 10 March 1999. 'I took Shabana to my village. My youngest sister was getting married. I made her meet everyone. It was also the time when the shooting for *Shool* (1999) was underway.'

'When Shabana came to participate in the wedding, their relationship became official. Manoj bhaiyya asked me to make her a part of every ritual. "She is a Muslim, and it shouldn't seem like we are discriminating against her," he told me. So, she participated in everything. She visited the temple too with us for the prayer service. In fact, when we visited Mumbai, it was Shabana who showed us around,' says Poonam.

It wasn't easy for a man from a traditional Brahmin family in Bihar to marry a Muslim girl, but everyone was aware of Manoj's persistent nature. The late Radhakant Bajpayee told me, 'We didn't say anything regarding marriage because this is how it happens in the film world.'

'My family might have been worried about Shabana's religion, but nobody expressed it openly. They didn't show any sadness either. On the other hand, Shabana's family was open and progressive. They were not opposed to interfaith marriage and they had made that abundantly clear.'

Harsh Chhaya was one of the close friends with whom Manoj had spoken about the possibility of a life with Shabana. Manoj took Shabana to meet Harsh and Shefali on Diwali. 'Manoj forbade me from calling many people as he was bringing Shabana for the first time. I couldn't say anything as it was about Shabana.

We have been close friends, so I was a bit hurt when I got to know of Manoj's wedding in the newspapers,' says Harsh.

Whatever be the reason behind it, Manoj and Shabana married in such haste that even Manoj's parents couldn't attend it. His late mother told me, 'We knew about Manoj and Shabana, but the wedding was planned suddenly. We had been to Mumbai a few days before his wedding to see his house. He didn't talk about marriage even then. Then he suddenly said that he was getting married. We asked him to have the wedding in the village, but he didn't agree to it.'

Manoj and Shabana were living together for a long time before they got married. They were very committed to each other from early on in their relationship. The need to legalize their relationship arose when they applied for a home loan. Shabana, in an interview with Ajay Brahmatmaj, said, 'Our families had accepted us. Now it was up to us to get married. Should I tell you why we got married? We had gone for a loan. The bank officer said we couldn't get the joint loan because we were not married. Other issues were also there in which a marriage certificate was needed. We were anyway going to get married, but such things increased the necessity. We thought even people ask bizarre questions, so let's shut them all up.'[31]

'We were having the best time of our bachelorhood and were together. We were thinking of marriage for two or three years, but somehow it kept getting delayed,' says Manoj.

Whatever be the reason, none of the two marriages could give Manoj family happiness in the way they wanted, basically the fun and frolic associated with the traditional Indian weddings. 'Whenever Maa visited Bhaiyya in Mumbai, she asked him to get married. "When she is the one taking care of everything, from the kitchen to the laundry, then you should marry her," she would tell him. But Bhaiyya always deflected the question. One day he said that they been married in the court of law,' says Poonam.

It was somewhere around 2004.

Religion didn't remain important in Manoj and Shabana's wedding. Bollywood, anyway, is known for being a cultural melting pot. It's a different thing that prejudices and upbringing impact the decision-making of such a couple. Manoj and Shabana passed this test with flying colours, thanks to their maturity and love for each other.

'We have our own set of religious beliefs and practices, but we don't interfere in each other's methods and faith,' says Shabana.

Chapter 16

From *Satya* to *Shool*

'The character I played in Shool *had a deep impact on my subconscious. My life was imbalanced. I had to seek a psychiatrist's help. I was also advised to stay away from acting for a few years.'*

Manoj and Ram Gopal Varma (Ramu) had grown close during the shooting of *Satya*. And this paved the way for two more amazing Hindi films: *Kaun* and *Shool*. They had also worked on a Telugu film titled *Prema Katha*. But after *Satya*, everybody expected more from the duo.

Kaun had only three characters, and it had no casting hassles. Sushant Singh had a small role in *Satya*, but Ramu had gauged his potential. So, he was given a substantial role in *Kaun*, the other two were Manoj and Urmila, Ramu's favourites.

Manoj wanted to play his character in *Kaun* in a different way. He couldn't convey his dilemma to Ramu because he had given Manoj his big break. He summoned the required courage before the first shot though. 'When I brought it up with Ramu, it was almost the shoot time. Ramu asked me to go for the shot. I insisted on showing him how I wanted to play the role. Upon seeing this, Ramu jumped for joy and permitted me to play the character the way I wanted to.'

Shool, which was set in Bihar, was the story of an honest policeman, for which Manoj was selected; rather it was written with him in mind.

Anurag Kashyap was supposed to direct *Shool*, but he stayed away from it due to creative differences with Ramu. However, Anurag, under Manoj's pressure, took the charge of film's writing and many other departments.

They needed such an actor as a villain who could counter Manoj Bajpayee's forceful presence and frame-domination. From Naseeruddin Shah to Amitabh Bachchan, many were considered, but none of them worked out. It was already a week into *Satya*'s release and the casting for *Shool* was going in full swing. An actor's photo in the *Times of India* caught Manoj's attention. It was Sayaji Shinde. Already famous in Marathi theatre, Shinde's story impressed Manoj. He obtained Shinde's number and called him at home. Shinde was out for his solo play *Tumbara* in Nagpur. 'I received a call from home that Manoj Bajpayee had called for some film,' remembers Shinde. 'I was returning to Mumbai after two days, so thought of talking to him then. I called Manoj Bajpayee upon my return. He said it's a Ram Gopal Varma film and asked me if I was willing to work in it. I readily agreed. Ramu finalized me after meeting me. I later got to know it was the main villain's role.'

Kaun's shooting was completed before the starting of the shooting for *Shool*. *Kaun* was mostly shot at night, and it was a seventeen–eighteen-day schedule. *Kaun* released in February 1999. It was different from what people expected from the collaboration of Ramu and Manoj after *Satya*. It was a suspense thriller with subtle dialogues. It was an experimental film with a bungalow as the prime location. There were three characters and no songs, unlike any Bollywood film. It was made on a limited budget, so it was loss proof, so to say. Critics praised the film for its unique content though. All three lead characters were praised for their acting. Anupama Chopra wrote in *India Today*, 'While Matondkar, all quivering lips and eyes wide with fear, is over the top, Bajpayee is bang on. Veering between a nerdy salesman-type and a deranged killer, he keeps up the tension.'[32]

The first schedule of *Shool* was shot in Bihar's Motihari. Because it was Manoj's home town, a crowd was expected and thus the makers arranged for a great security circle. Then there was superstar Raveena Tandon's craze, everybody wanted to get a glimpse of her. Manoj's mother gave the first clap of *Shool* in the Motihari schedule.

Manoj has narrated one particular story related to *Shool*'s shooting at many places. 'I was shooting with Raveena at the Motihari railway station. My friends came to meet me where I was staying. They wanted to meet Raveena too. I cited security concerns for Raveena and said that it would be very difficult for me. They abused me and said what good was it me being the hero of the film if they can't even meet Raveena.'

Not only friends, family members were also ecstatic about watching a big Bollywood film shoot. After all, the first born of the house was shooting in the vicinity and the newspapers were carrying the news every day. 'I had forbidden my family members from coming to the shoot, because I feared if somebody misbehaved with them in the crowd, I would feel bad. However, when I was shooting, I saw my father in the crowd. I gestured him to go back and he signalled agreement, as if to tell me that, "You carry on with your work." I got to know later he was there to see Raveena Tandon!'

That was a notorious time in Bihar's history. Musclemen called the shots in the Lalu Yadav era. Yashpal Sharma, who played an important character in *Shool*, said on a TV show, 'Manoj was expected to hold a country-made pistol in one scene. The director asked the spot boy to bring one, but by the time he could return, one person in the crowd pulled out a pistol from under his shirt and asked whether this would work. We were shocked, to say the least.'

Bihar was notorious for crime then. So, the state government provided a four-layer security to Raveena. She later told Manoj that she had felt like Indira Gandhi with such a security cover.

As Inspector Samar Pratap Singh, Manoj was in top form in *Shool*. In fact, many rate it as his finest performance. '*Shool* was shot near our village and I was there and one day Bhaiyya scolded me like anything. One day I saw him pacing up and down in deep concentration. I asked him to sit when I saw him. He screamed at me in a sharp voice. Later when he went for the shot, I realized he was in his character and was trying to bring out the aggression needed for it. I probably disturbed his thought process, which irked him,' recalls Manoj's sister Garima.

Manoj had imbibed the character of Samar Pratap to such an extent that it impacted the flow of his thoughts. His life was imbalanced, and he had to seek psychiatric help. The critics went gaga over his acting in *Shool*. It was also impressive the way Raveena shed her glamorous image and ditched make-up for a power-packed performance. Her work in *Shool* was commendable. Some newspapers called *Shool* Raveena's attempt at art films. Raveena had also answered the question in an interview, '*Shool* is not an art film but a serious film, and I want to do such films which could give me satisfaction. Working with Manoj Bajpayee gave me immense pleasure. I think he is one of the finest actors in the industry. He is an actor in true senses, not a star, who beats up ten–twelve people.'[33]

Manoj Bajpayee received the Filmfare Best Actor (Critics) award for *Shool*. He got emotional while receiving the award. 'People said *Shool* is not popular. Last time they said Bhiku Mhatre is not popular. For me, what was important was the Filmfare documentary that was shown before the film. In it, there were stars, who are either sitting in front of me or are with me on the dais, who were shown entering the auditorium. I thought then if I ever would be there and when this 'lady' will be in my hands without any make-up. I have gotten the chance this year as well. I first want to thank Amitabh Bachchan. Amitji, I tried a lot, but I think I couldn't give what you have done in *Zanjeer*, because of which I am here. Thank you, Amitji. I also want to thank the people of Bihar. I went to shoot there, and no untoward incident happened, for which Bihar keeps hitting the headlines. I am proud of Bihar and its people.'[34]

Nawazuddin Siddiqui had also played a minor role in *Shool*; it was his second film. Anurag Kashyap did not want Nawazuddin to settle for a small role; Nawazuddin needed the money. It was a similar situation to that when Manoj requested Ramu for a role in *Daud* for the money. It's a different matter that Nawazuddin never received the payment for the role. 'Never got any payment, but we kept going and eating at Ramu's office for six months.'

The commercial failure of *Kaun* and *Shool* might not have made Manoj a typical Bollywood star, but these two, along with *Satya*, established him as an actor.

In the same year, 1999, Shabana's *Hogi Pyaar ki Jeet* hit the screens. It also had Ajay Devgn, Arshad Warsi and Mayuri Kango in the lead roles. It didn't make any heads turn and Shabana's acting career took a severe hit.

Meanwhile, some filmmakers started planning scripts keeping Manoj in mind. One such film was *Dil Pe Mat Le Yaar!* (2000).

Chapter 17

A Fragile Heart

'I formed a company called Talking Pictures and went to Manoj with a Rs 51,000 cheque. I asked him to sign the film because I had become the producer. He did.'

Manoj made two important films of his career after *Shool*: *Ghaath* and *Dil Pe Mat Le Yaar!*. While *Ghaath* released in December 2000, *Dil Pe Mat Le Yaar!* hit the screens in September 2000. Not only was Manoj playing the lead roles in them, but they were also made as per the commercial formula, with action, emotion, songs, dances, one-liners etc.

While Akashdeep Sabir was the director of *Ghaath*, *Dil Pe Mat Le Yaar!* was helmed by Hansal Mehta. *Ghaath* brought Manoj and Irrfan, who played a corrupt builder, together. They meet on-screen in the first or second scene itself when Irrfan, with his henchmen, comes to vacate Manoj's chawl.

The opening scene itself sets the mood for the movie.

Manoj did a song sequence in the film in which he had to dance shirtless with Tabu, but it still bombed at the box office. However, his friendship with Tabu is still intact. He calls her by her nickname 'Tabban'. 'Manoj was really shy those days. I occasionally came up with ideas to poke him. Sometimes I deliberately flirted with him. Once during a shoot at the Filmalaya Studios, I entered his van. He was so bewildered, I thought he would jump out of the van,' Tabu reveals.

Dil Pe Mat Le Yaar! released before *Ghaath*. Manoj valued his relationships with some industry folks more than films. However, not everything went right.

I am not clear who the original idea belonged to. Saurabh Shukla told me it was his idea, while Hansal Mehta claimed it was his idea that originated from the news of Gulshan Kumar's murder. As per Hansal, he wanted to peek into the mind of Gulshan Kumar's murderer.

Hansal had written a blog centred around *Dil Pe Mat Le Yaar!*. 'I narrated the idea to Manoj Bajpayee and Anurag Kashyap. It was probably during the shoot of *Satya*. We were drinking that day. In the state of inebriation, I signed them with a significant amount of Re 1. We decided we will make a film and we continued drinking.'[35]

At that time, Hansal was making *Jayate* (1997), which was Anurag's first film as a writer. This project never saw the light of day. On the other hand, *Satya* turned out to be a superhit. Manoj and Anurag had become a star actor and writer, respectively. Anurag was associated with *Kaun* and *Shool* too. He was planning to direct his first film, tentatively titled *Mirage*, which was later renamed *Paanch* (2003).

Manoj didn't have any dearth of offers after *Satya*. Many producers reached his doorstep with briefcases full of cash. 'After *Satya*, a producer from Bihar reached out to me. He wanted to sign Manoj for a film and wanted me to put him in touch with Manoj. He was willing to make an offer of Rs 30 lakh in cash! When I got in touch with Manoj, he said he wasn't interested in such projects. He quoted Rs 70 lakh for the film just so he could avoid the producer,' recalls Vineet Kumar.

Meanwhile, due to the non-release of *Jayate*, Hansal had to go back to television. While filming an episode called *Ae Mote* for the 'Rishtey' series on Zee TV, Hansal discussed *Dil Pe Mat Le Yaar!* with Saurabh Shukla. Saurabh wrote the film for free. But he wanted to play the character of the videographer in the film. Then they started to look for the producer. The budget was an estimated Rs 20 lakh.

'Owing to Saurabh's efforts, we found a producer. We wanted to shoot on 16mm. The only condition the producer had was that only Manoj Bajpayee would do the role of Ram Saran. Then our worst fear came true. Manoj refused to do the role. He wanted to be a part of a big film. He wanted to help me out, but in a big-banner film,' says Hansal.

Hansal was getting anxious. He decided to produce the film himself. Anish Ranjan came forward to offer his help. Anish wanted to be an independent producer. He shared his plan with Manoj, but Manoj believed Anish should gain experience in other departments related to film-making before getting into production.

'One guy from Bihar was ready to invest money in the film, and he wanted me to be the producer,' says Anish. 'In between came the *Dil Pe Mat Le Yaar!* project that Manoj liked but was stuck due to finances. I formed a company called Talking Pictures and went to Manoj with a cheque of Rs 51,000. I asked him to sign the film because I had become the producer. He did. We had a party that night. During the conversation I asked Manoj about his fees. He asked me to touch base with his secretary Bhaskar Shetty about the money. I called Bhaskar the next day. He was aware that Manoj and I were friends. I asked him to forget friendship and put himself in my place and then quote a price. He said since Manoj got Rs 20 lakh for *Ghaath*, he should be getting Rs 25 lakh for this one. I agreed to the amount but told him that I would be getting back to him with when and how the money is to be paid.'

Hansal Mehta made a film of his liking. Harsh Chhaya also played an important character in it. Harsh was recommended by Manoj. '*Dil Pe Mat Le Yaar!* was either my first or second film. Shefali and I had already separated by then. Manoj was concerned and wanted to put me to work. Some people have always been in my life through thick and thin. They have been emotionally attached to me. Manoj and Vineet Kumar were such people,' says Harsh.

Choreographer Remo D'Souza started his career with this film.

Manoj had to go abroad for the shooting of *Aks* (2001) before the release of *Dil Pe Mat Le Yaar!*. *Aks* was his first big project with Amitabh Bachchan. A screening of *Dil Pe Mat Le Yaar!* was organized in Mumbai where Sridevi, Jaya Bachchan, Ram Gopal Varma and other celebrities made their presence felt. Shabana, along with her mother, had also come for the screening. Anish Ranjan remembers it being very crowded. 'I asked Shabana many times to grab her seat, but she didn't listen. She didn't complain to me, but later I got to know that she had a problem finding a seat. When Manoj found out about it, he gave Hansal an earful over the phone.'

Everyone—Manoj, Hansal and Anish—took the incident to their hearts in different ways. Some people associated with the film said there was a strained exchange between Saurabh Shukla and Manoj as well. However, Saurabh clarified saying that: 'It's not like I never had any differences with Manoj, but it can't be called a fight.'

Hansal wrote on his blog, 'I paid the price of the film with my friendship with Manoj Bajpayee. Probably passion has its own price.'[36]

Anish Ranjan must have felt bad about his childhood friendship breaking up in such a manner.

I asked Anish if the fallout with Manoj happened because he had become a producer.

He said, 'It was probably bound to happen even if I wasn't a producer. We couldn't give each other enough time at that point in our careers. Manoj believed I was ignoring him and giving more importance to Hansal and others.'

Dil Pe Mat Le Yaar! didn't work at the box office. Had it been a hit, the commercial aspect of the friendship could have taken over. But as they say, time heals everything. Years later, Manoj did one of the best films of his career under Hansal Mehta's direction: *Aligarh.*

They were back on talking terms during the shooting of Sanjay Gupta's *Dus Kahaniyaan* (2007), though. 'We didn't talk to each other for six years. Our relationship was so strained that if we ever crossed paths, we would look the other way,' says Hansal. 'Then we met at Sanjay Gupta's house for *Dus Kahaniyaan*. I had to talk to him for commercial reasons. We met for drinks after the shoot. Sat together. We wondered why we had stopped talking to each other for so many years. It was a stupid fight.'

'Hansal had kept a party for *Aligarh*. When I reached, Manoj came to the gate to receive me. Then he took me to meet everyone.' Anish recalls.

It's indeed difficult not to take certain things to heart!

Chapter 18

A Decade of Hopelessness

'I had been in theatre for many years. I believed that bad times too shall pass. But how do I make that happen? I rediscovered myself. Learnt pranayama, meditation, started going back to Delhi and to my village, read a lot of books, organized workshops and utilized the bad time for the preparation of good times.'

The first decade of the new millennium was fruitless for Manoj Bajpayee, who had created history right before it started. Not that he selected all the bad films or acted badly in them, but 90 per cent of those projects failed to earn money. This is the harsh reality of commercial cinema. If you can't make money, you do not get many backers.

Among the films that did work, it is only the success of *Raajneeti* (2010) that can be credited to Manoj to some extent. It was a multi-starrer anyway. Manoj was a hot property when *Aks* released in 2001. He was playing a villain against the superstar of the millennium—Amitabh Bachchan. 'This film earned me respect. I will rate it among the fifty best films of the last five decades. This character needed me to go through a particular thought process. I asked Rakeysh Omprakash Mehra as to what role I would be playing. "Demon," he said.'

Aks and Anubhav Sinha's *Tum Bin* released on the same day— 13 July 2001. It was a David versus Goliath match. 'I remember noted critic Khalid Mohamed had heavily praised *Aks* and called *Tum Bin* "Tum Thin",' says Anubhav Sinha. In India, the critics don't get the pulse of the audience all the time. While *Aks* bombed, *Tum Bin* turned out to be a sleeper hit.

Amitabh Bachchan and Manoj Bajpayee struck a bond during the shooting of *Aks* which was informal yet respectful. Manoj told a story on *The Kapil Sharma Show*. 'Amitji and I were expected to jump from a height of 100 feet for one of the scenes. I was anxious as I am very scared of heights. I asked the action director to remove the scene, but he didn't agree to do so. He tried to infuse spirit in me by saying that, "Amitji is also there with you in the scene, you relax." We started climbing and Amitji kept pepping me up. When we climbed around 80 feet, he said, "Manoj if something happens to me . . ." I became even more nervous. I said, "Sir, I am anyway very scared!" He continued, "If something happens to me, just inform Jaya that . . ." Then he started laughing. It was just a prank, but it scared the daylights out of me.'

The late Radhakantji also told me a story. 'We were in Mumbai. One day, Manoj sent a vehicle and called us to the studio. A big van was standing there. The driver told us Amitabh Bachchan was inside. Chairs were brought for us. Suddenly, there was a noise about a shot being ready. Amitji got out of his van, and everyone started looking towards him. It felt that the president was coming. When he came closer, he greeted Manoj and asked how he was. His voice is anyway incredible. When Manoj told him about us, he asked for us. Upon seeing us, he bent down and touched our feet. It seemed he knew Manoj for long. Abhishek Bachchan also reached there around the same time. Amitji called him as well and he also touched our feet. Amitji said, "Babusahab [Abhishek] has just returned from foreign after completing his studies." We talked for a few minutes and then he left for his shot.'

Zubeidaa released in 2001. It was directed by the pioneer of the parallel cinema in Bollywood—Shyam Benegal. It wasn't an art film. Manoj was cast as a prince. He was cast with a young star like Karisma Kapoor and a stalwart like Rekha. The story was written by Khalid Mohamed, who wrote in *Khaleej Times*, 'Anil Kapoor and Aamir Khan had rejected the film, because they thought it was woman-centric.'[37]

However, Shyam Benegal had faith in Manoj. Many associated with the project objected to Manoj playing the lead role, but Benegal went ahead with him. Khalid Mohamed wrote, 'The maharajas and princes of Rajasthan don't look like our Bollywood heroes. They aren't fair-complexioned or handsome in the conventional sense of the word. Actually, there's something extraordinary about Manoj's deep-set eyes, which he uses very expressively.'[38]

Even Manoj was surprised to be chosen as a prince. 'I was surprised when Shyam Benegal asked me to play a prince in *Zubeidaa*. My instinctive reaction was to refuse the film because I didn't want people to blame Shyam Babu for wrong casting, but Shyam Babu was adamant. He called me to his office and showed me pictures of many royal families; they all looked like me, like any ordinary person. Once that fear was out of the way, I enjoyed playing my character and the experience of shooting with two terrific actresses, Rekhaji and Karisma, was unforgettable. It was because of *Zubeidaa* that Yash Chopra offered me the musical romance *Veer-Zaara* (2004).'

Zubeidaa won the National Award for Best Feature film in 2000, but it failed commercially. Manoj's achievement was working with people like Rekha and Shyam Benegal. Rekha played Manoj's wife in the film. It was a unique experience. Manoj, in an interview with *Navbharat Times*, said, 'She played my wife who's older than me and she used to teach me things about etiquette of how to hold the hand of a lady. Horse riding is something I will always remember. I used to go from Lokhandwala to Race Course every day at 5.30 a.m. Most of the polo scenes are done by me. Playing polo is child's play.'[39]

Manoj was seen in just one film in 2002: the Rajat Mukherjee-directed *Road*. Produced by Ram Gopal Varma, it saw Manoj as a serial killer. This not only bombed at the ticket window, but critics also panned Manoj. Sukanya Verma of Rediff wrote, 'Touted as the surprise package of *Road*, Manoj Bajpayee is a letdown. He hams, uses his previous negative performances in *Kaun* and *Aks* to irritating effect here. The actor is in serious danger of turning into a caricature.'[40]

In 2003, Manoj had only two releases: Chandraprakash Dwivedi's *Pinjar* and J.P. Dutta's *LOC: Kargil. Pinjar* was based on Amrita Pritam's novel of the same name. He played the character of Rashid with such intensity that he won the 2004 National Award (Special Jury) for the film. Manoj, in an interview, said, 'It was a difficult role because it starts with negativity, and the audience begin to hate him; this is the journey of the character. In the end, it was difficult to win over Urmila's character and the viewers. I tried to give my best. I remember I ran towards my vanity after every scene. I read the ten scenes before and after every scene many times to understand the right graph and hit correct chords. Each shot was a challenge.'[41]

Pinjar didn't work at the ticket window, and it resulted in eight months of unemployment for Manoj. All he was offered were roles of traditional villains, which he wanted to stay away from. He was also offered a Hollywood film with American actress Viola Lynn Collins. 'I had gone to Jaisalmer for a film project. I met renowned actor Shrivallabh Vyas's father, who was a famous astrologer. He was very old and spoke with difficulty. I asked him what will happen to this international project. He said nothing. I insisted him to look again. He repeated: "Nothing is going to happen." I returned. I was in two minds. Eventually, we returned after finishing the shoot and nothing happened.'[42]

Such incidents made his belief in astrology stronger, so much so that he himself studies the subject now. Many of his friends and acquaintances seek his advice from time to time. 'I have had an interest in astrology since childhood. I have studied it. But when I met my Gurubhai, Anand Acharya, I understood the depth of the matter. I met my spiritual teacher through Anand. He taught me how to control my temper. I am happy I met Guruji, but at the same time I regret not having met him twenty years ago.' (I also have a story here. When I told Manoj about my company Jyotish Application AstroSage Kundli, he said he already had it on his phone!)

LOC: Kargil released in December 2003. It had a massive starcast: Sanjay Dutt, Suniel Shetty, Ajay Devgn, Abhishek Bachchan, Ashutosh Rana, Akshaye Khanna and, of course, Manoj Bajpayee. Since there were many actors in the film, Manoj and Ashutosh had to improvise at a couple of places. *LOC* received an average return at the box office.

Manoj also worked in Makarand Deshpande's directorial debut *Hanan* (2004). 'Manoj played the role of a mad person in my film *Hanan*, which has many shades. Unfortunately, the film was never released. Had it been released, he would have won awards,' says Makarand. Manoj played a dacoit in the film who settles down in a village after killing many people as a mad man. He gets married to Sonali Kulkarni in the film. Makarand also played a pivotal role. The film is now available on YouTube.

Manoj had two more flops in 2004: *Jaago* and *Inteqam*. *Jaago* was directed by Mehul Kumar. The film dealt with the subject of rape, but in a very mainstream Bollywood way. *Inteqam* was directed by Pankaj Parashar, who had thrown Manoj out of *Ab Aayega Maza* citing bad acting. 'I told Bhaiyya not to do any similar film after watching it. It doesn't suit his character,' comments Manoj's youngest sister, Garima.

Manoj expressed the wish to work with Yash Chopra and in return bagged a small but important role in *Veer-Zaara*. It was the role of Preity Zinta's fiancé, Raza Shirazi. He hardly had three scenes, but he left his mark. Jitesh Pillai wrote in the *Times of India*, 'Manoj Bajpayee's short but silken menace has the desired effect.'[43] *Veer-Zaara* was a superhit. He also gained an identity overseas.

Another plus point was that Manoj got to work with his old friend Shah Rukh Khan. Enough has been written about their equation and the time they spent at Barry John's theatre workshops, but there was more to them than just acting together. 'Manoj and Shah Rukh share a normal relationship. Everybody had a lobby then—English speaking and Hindi speaking. But everybody mixed well on the sets,' Manoj's old friend Sanjay Sujitabh says.

Manoj and Shah Rukh shared a camaraderie. In fact, the first time Manoj went to a disco, it was with Shah Rukh.

It was one of the poshest discos of Delhi, situated in Maurya Sheraton where the country's first female DJ Nalini (Field Marshal K.M. Cariappa's daughter) played. In the group, Shah Rukh had a Maruti van and Rituraj had a Maruti 800. Ghungroo was a unique experience for someone like Manoj who was struggling for bread and work. Manoj, in an interview, said, 'I went to a disco called Ghungroo with Shah Rukh and other friends. I was wearing slippers and the manager didn't allow me inside. Shah Rukh and a few other friends went to the hotel and borrowed a pair of shoes for me from the hotel staff. Eventually, we reached the disco. Living with English-speaking people like Shah Rukh actually helped.'[44]

'He was always the centre of attraction. We were considered good actors, but nobody sat with us. Girls always wanted to be with him,' says Manoj.

Shah Rukh got busy with television shows when Manoj was doing theatre, and he was already a superstar when Manoj reached Mumbai. Manoj said in an interview with Atika Ahmad Farooqui, 'I am really proud of Shah Rukh and his achievements, probably more than my own achievements, because he didn't have anyone. Neither parents nor anybody else. Today he has a big family. I became what I set out for, and he achieved what he had to. We were very clear about goals.'[45]

Once Shah Rukh was asked to deliver a monologue at the Barry John workshop. He gave a speech as a superstar. 'I [Manoj] never wanted to have the superstar tag. If it was like that, I wouldn't have done *Kaun* after *Satya*. Wouldn't have done films such as *Shool*, *Zubeidaa* or *Pinjar* after *Kaun*. Such films don't make you a star but establish you as an artist. My films make my intentions clear.'

It's also true that whenever Manoj dabbled in pure commercial films, he met with failure. One such role was Dharmesh Darshan's *Bewafaa* (2005). His role was edited out and he wasn't very happy about it. He also worked in the Deepak Tijori-directed crime thriller *Fareb* (2005) with the Shetty sisters—Shilpa and Shamita. He also appeared in an English film titled *Return to Rajapur* (2006). It was shown at the New York Film Festival, but it couldn't create any impact on the Indian audience due to limited release. Based in Rajasthan, it was about an Indian prince who runs a heritage hotel.

The year 2005 was particularly bad for him, but during all this, one film gave him some solace. It was *1971* (2007), which was directed by the legendary Ramanand Sagar's grandson, Amrit Sagar. From the germ of the idea to winning the National Award, the story of *1971* calls for a separate chapter, but in short, it was a film that resurfaced years later to find its audience.

Amrit had met Manoj with his script for *Paint* in 2004. It didn't work out, but they agreed to meet again with a new story. Amrit had a short story titled *Six Prisoners*, which was written by his father Motilal Sagar in 1972. This one was about the hardships faced by the prisoners of war against the backdrop of the India–Pakistan wars.

'The moment Manoj heard the story, he said this is the film I should make. I said this will require a lot of money as it's going to be a big film. He said no film is big or small, it's only good or bad. "But how do I develop the idea?" I asked him. He said he was an equally driven person and that we would all strike it well,' shares Amrit.

Manoj arranged for a meeting between Amrit and Piyush Mishra, who had recently shifted to Mumbai and was looking for work. Piyush himself has confirmed that he got *1971* on Manoj's recommendation.

Piyush and Amrit wrote the film together. Then a location was finalized near Manali. 'Manoj was our final choice,' adds Amrit. 'We contacted Jimmy Shergill for the role of Flight Lt Ram, but he refused. Then came Deepak Dobriyal. Piyush had brought him in, it was his first film. Ravi Kishan met us at Natraj Studio. We knew him from Bhojpuri films, and he wanted to be given a chance. We were impressed with his screen test. Actors like Kumud Mishra and Manav Kaul also joined the cast.'

'There was no heroine in *1971*. The shooting for the film started in Manali in the month of April 2005. The weather was our adversary because of the high altitude.'

'The film has a scene in which Manoj, Manav, Ravi and Deepak cross the jungle in a vehicle. Manav started the car but put extra pressure on the accelerator and it headed towards a deep trench of 100 feet. The vehicle somehow stopped due to a small rock, otherwise something untoward could have happened that day,' recalls Amrit.

'We had a real blast during the shooting of the film,' says Ravi, looking back on those days. 'We were like kids again. It was the first film that I worked in which had no heroines. We would pull Manoj's leg because he always woke up very early in the morning, like a village oldie. Truthfully, *1971* got made because of the collective passion of Manoj, Piyush and Amrit. And that incident with the vehicle was seriously scary!'

Manoj's legs would be absolutely numb due to the running around in the snow during the climax shoot of *1971*. 'His knees were troubling him,' remembers Amrit. 'He faced difficulty in running, and he was supposed to run a lot in the snow during the climax. We somehow managed for one day. But that night, Manoj came to my room. He was in pain, warming his cramped knees. I was worried, since I did not have another climax in mind. But I was not oblivious to Manoj's evident discomfort. I asked Manoj what to do, if Suraj Singh's character was unable to run in the end. Should he be shot dead without even attempting to run? I was considering various alternatives, but Manoj was adamant that he will run, whatever the situation be.'

'I can never forget those sixty days of the shoot. I almost died, twice,' says Manoj.

The shooting of the film was completed in 2005, but it released in 2007.

In 2006, Manoj had just one release: *Happy*, which was in Telugu.

Manoj had high hopes from *1971*, but every film has its own journey. Unfortunately, this one couldn't get the kind of release it deserved. The day it hit the theatres, half-a-dozen other films also released. When Amrit went to watch the film at a theatre in Mumbai with a friend, there were just two people—only them. He was heartbroken. It wasn't only his debut, but the latest in the legacy of family productions. On top of everything, his father was the producer, so much expectation was pinned on him.

One day, Manoj called up Amrit and said he should send the film for the National Award. When the National Awards were not announced in 2008, Amrit forgot about it. But it won the National Award for Best Film in 2009. However, it couldn't reach the wider audience and it pinched Manoj, Amrit and the others who were involved in the film.

The film came back into prominence during the Covid-induced lockdown of 2020. Somebody expressed the desire to watch *1971* on Twitter (now X). Manoj tagged Amrit in the tweet, who put the film out on YouTube. It simply started a chain reaction, and more than 20 million people watched the film in the first forty-five days. It was a film that went viral after thirteen years of its release. Had it received a proper release in 2007, who knows where the film would have been!

Manoj also acted with Juhi Chawla in *Swami* (2007), which was directed by choreographer Ganesh Acharya. This one failed as well. He was seen with Dia Mirza in one of the stories of *Dus Kahaniyaan*, which also tanked at the box office.

Rediff.com wrote about *Swami*: 'Bajpayee is brilliant as the small-town man who moves to the city and goes through the amazing journey of life with its ups and downs. His sincere portrayal of a regular middle-class man will touch many hearts.'[46]

Manoj did a comedy film titled *Money Hai Toh Honey Hai* (2008) with Govinda. By this time, Manoj's health was beginning to hamper his work. His eyes too were troubling him. Ravi Kishan recalls that when they were in Mauritius to shot *Money Hai Toh Honey Hai*, Manoj always had a hanky as his eyes would be constantly teary.

By this time in his career, there was a common allegation against Manoj that he poked his nose in the director's work. In his defence, this is what he had to say: 'I surrendered myself to Ganesh on the sets. I have learnt my lesson. I don't give advice till the time I am asked to. I am facing unnecessary allegations of interference while all I am trying to do is to better the team product. My New Year resolution is to focus on my own work and leave everything else to the producer and director.'

The year 2009 saw the release of *Jugaad*, *Acid Factory* and *Jail*, but they too flopped. Shabana Raza had a small part in *Acid Factory*, the only film after *Fiza* in which she and Manoj worked together.

Manoj had told me a story from the shooting of *Jugaad*. 'It is such a small-budget film that when a crowd was required for a scene, the producer went to the nearby factory and spread the rumour about Kareena Kapoor shooting there. All the workers came to see her, and we captured them as a crowd.' He was seen with Irrfan for the second time in *Acid Factory*, though it was just one scene.

Neil Nitin Mukesh was in the lead and Manoj was in a supporting role in Madhur Bhandarkar's *Jail*. Manoj walked the ramp for the first time for a film's publicity. He accepted publicity as an integral part of film-making. He called me up and dictated a long blog post. It read, 'When I stepped on the ramp for the promotion of *Jail*, many questioned if this is the new fashion trend for film actors? Will such a tactic ensure the film's success? Probably this was asked recurringly because all the members of the *Jail* cast—Neil, Mugdha, Madhur Bhandarkar and I—walked the ramp together. Neil and I also had handcuffs and jail uniform on. The point is not walking the ramp, but the questions asked about it. There's no doubt a ramp walk has become a part of the film promotion. In the age of consumerism, film is also a product and Bollywood has understood it. Like a product, films also need advertising. Many can question whether publicity can make a film a hit. Because we have seen many hugely publicized films not making a mark at the box office. There's no doubt that publicity is not everything, but it is still important. The audience should know about a new release, its actors, its story; only then will they take the trouble to go to the halls. I didn't value publicity as important in the beginning of my career, but now I have realized that I was wrong. I have seen the result of bad publicity. My film *Swami* was praised by critics, but it flopped because nobody knew when it hit the theatres. I believe *1971* is the best film of my career. It received the National Award for Best Hindi Feature Film. Due to the lack of publicity, not many people turned up to watch the film.. I have the same opinion about the recently released *Acid Factory* that it wasn't promoted well. So, is there no place for word-of-mouth publicity? My answer is no. The film business is about three days now and if the audience reached theatres in those three days. Next week, 3–4 more films are ready for the release.'[47]

Manoj's arguments were not wrong, but it's also true that he did films like *Jugaad* and *Jail* because he needed the money. In 2009, one thing that got going for him was the inclusion in Prakash Jha's multi-starrer *Raajneeti*. Interestingly, he found the film because Irrfan decided not to do it. 'I contacted Irrfan first for the character of Virendra Pratap,' says Jha. 'He said he wanted to do the lead role. It didn't work out. I have been wanting to work with Manoj for a very long time. When I narrated the role to him, he liked it. It had many shades. Also, Manoj is an artist, not a hero. He understands reasoning. He grabbed it with both hands and worked on the role. He is from theatre and works with a lot of back-end work. Like Shabana Azmi, he too asks a lot of questions. My working style is that I narrate the role to the actor and ask them to prepare its backstory.'

Raajneeti released in 2010. The hit dialogue '*Karara jawab milega*' [You will get a crisp reply] reminded everyone of '*Mumbai ka King kaun?*' Manoj's journalist friend Anuranjan Jha says, 'Manoj had gone to my village for an event. When he was asked to say his famous dialogues, he said he would perform a new one, from a film that's not released. When he delivered that dialogue, people were clapping for a long time.'

Prakash Jha wanted to chop off the scene involving Manoj's famous dialogue due to the length of the film, but his team insisted on keeping it.

Manoj himself believed *Raajneeti* changed his career's path. He said in an interview, 'My health and career were going through a bad patch. I worked in Madhur Bhandarkar's *Jail*, but it didn't work. Every day was getting tougher. Then came *Raajneeti* and people's expectations started growing again. A hit film means a lot in this industry.'[48]

Manoj's performance in *Raajneeti* was appreciated by the audience and critics alike. It also started a new relationship with Prakash Jha, which had never found a solid ground before. Manoj defined this phase of his career candidly. 'From *Satya* to *Pinjar*, I had the trust of the people and was successful. Everything that could liberate me to work freely. Imagine, people work as per a commercial formula, but I worked as per my beliefs. I was stubborn and enjoying it. Then things started changing. My contemporaries like Kay Kay Menon and Irrfan were working with Vishal Bhardwaj and Anurag Kashyap. They were getting much hype. Their films were working in between, but mine were simply not working. So, there was no need of Manoj Bajpayee. Because he was not alone now, there were other actors like him with commercial advantages. I got sidelined. I was not depressed because I knew that this is how the industry functions. If you can't bring profits for the producer, the people running the business will remove you. Nobody is anybody's enemy here. If you can give a return on investment, you're considered good. If you can't, then people refuse to recognize you. I was suffering from a lot of health issues as well. My hand stopped working because of the ailing bone. My eyes were watery due to the closing of ducts. Some big doctors wanted to operate upon my shoulders, but my personal physiotherapist and doctor were not ready for it. One year went in vain. The occasional roles I was getting didn't excite me. All the good roles were going to either Kay Kay or Irrfan. I worked during that phase mostly to make ends meet.'

Sometimes I wonder if Manoj had such close relationships with good directors like Vishal Bhardwaj, Anurag Kashyap, Tigmanshu Dhulia and Anubhav Sinha, then why didn't he work with them earlier? Was he not offered good roles? Or was it an ego tussle?

'I had a plan of making a film with Manoj after *Satya*,' says Anubhav Sinha, 'but then we had some trouble with the dates. I didn't like something he had said and called off the project. Now that I think about it, I feel like even Manoj had little control over what was happening in his life during those days. Once you become a star, your life begins to get heavily influenced by a lot of people. But since we were old friends, we believed we had greater authority on his time and life. However, looking back, I feel we gravely misunderstood him.'

Anurag Kashyap revealed more about the incident Anubhav hinted at. 'Irrfan was on TV and none of his mainstream films had been released till then. One day we were all drinking and Manoj said something to the effect that, "You all want to be directors while riding on my shoulders." All four of us—Anubhav, Tigmanshu, Vishal and I—felt really bad about it. Then we all made our first films with somebody else.'

It's true all the close friends had just one star in their reach, and it was Manoj, so it was natural for them to make plans while keeping Manoj in the centre. However, the films chosen by Manoj were also questionable projects. 'A perception was created that I am an arrogant man, whose mind is corrupted by success. I was reading all this and understood that the next few years wouldn't be easy. So, I told myself that people are free to think what they want, but I am not letting go of this opportunity. I am going to walk the path I have chosen for myself. I was walking with blinders on and making many people unhappy on my way.'

When Manoj was working for money, one incident hurt him immensely. Shabana Raza had gone to a theatre to watch a film where only three girls were present. Their nasty comments irked Shabana big time. 'She called up after coming out of the theatre and said the film was indeed bad, but the way those three girls commented was disrespectful. "I only have one request, you don't work for only money. We will do something but not like this." Then I decided to not do bad films for the sake of money.'

I asked Manoj Bajpayee the name of the film he was referring to. He didn't give a clear-cut answer, but hinted towards a film called *Fareb*. Directed by Deepak Tijori, the film featured Manoj Bajpayee, Shamita Shetty and Shilpa Shetty in the lead roles.

Manoj needed the money for their dream house. The dream came true for Manoj and Shabana in 2008 when they purchased a huge house in Oberoi Towers. Frankly speaking, in between 2001 and 2010, Manoj Bajpayee's life had very few achievements.

Professionally, it was his winning the National Award for *Pinjar* and the box-office success of *Raajneeti*. Personally, it was his marriage to Shabana and buying a house. He didn't run away even in the dismal times in his career though. 'I had done theatre for many years. I believed this bad time too shall pass. But how do I make it happen? I rediscovered myself. Learnt pranayama, did meditation, started going back to Delhi and my village, read a lot of books, organized workshops and utilized the bad time for the preparation of good times.'

Chapter 19

Of Friends and Frenemies

'The problem with Ram Gopal Varma has been that he always wanted Manoj Bajpayee as an actor who can flatter him all the time. He wanted someone who has no self-respect. I just want to say that Mr Varma, please stop maligning my character.'

The new millennium didn't only harm Manoj professionally, but he also lost emotional attachment with many friends. For example, Anish Ranjan, Harsh Chhaya, Vijay Raj and Hansal Mehta. The problems with two particular people grew so much that they swore not to work with each other—Ram Gopal Varma and Anurag Kashyap.

The issues with Ramu

A hypothetical question that keeps doing the rounds is: what if Ramu hadn't given *Satya* to Manoj? Well, the answer is also hypothetical. Manoj's time had arrived, and he would have made his mark anyhow, with or without *Satya*. If not Ramu, some other able director would have given him a solid role. He had nearly fifteen years of acting experience and was waiting to explode. His *'achche din'* (good days) were just around the corner, and like Lord Ram, he had already lived fourteen years in *vanvaas*, or exile.

It's also true that many talents in Bollywood fail to achieve anything in the absence of a good project, so Ramu, in a way, played the perfect connoisseur for an uncut diamond like Manoj. After all, Manoj had come for a small role in *Daud*. However, even if he was not given the prominent role in *Satya*, Manoj would have still been identified as a good character artist. Manoj, as per some critics, is an actor in Naseeruddin Shah's league and is definitely among the best in the country. So, it's like believing in destiny and working to believe in destiny. The result would have been the same in both the cases.

After *Daud*, Manoj became an integral part of Ramu's Factory. He did *Prema Katha* in Telugu and *Shool*, *Kaun* and *Road* in Hindi. But then they had such a rift that they never worked together again. But what exactly was the reason behind such a tiff?

One reason was Manoj not getting any role in many Ram Gopal Varma films. After *Road* in 2002 till *Ram Gopal Varma ki Aag* (2007), he made many Hindi films: *Bhoot* (2003), *Darna Mana Hai* (2003), *Main Madhuri Dixit Banna Chahti Hoon* (2003), *Ek Haseena Thi* (2002), *Ab Tak Chhappan* (2004), *Gayab* (2004), *Vaastu Shastra* (2004), *Naach* (2004), *D* (2005), *Sarkar* (2005), *My Wife's Murder* (2005), *James* (2005), *Mr Ya Miss* (2005), *Darna Zaroori Hai* (2006) and *Nishabd* (2007). Many of these were experimental films where Manoj could have fit in. It's not like Manoj was not talking to Ramu. Manoj has given ample hints in his blog dated 11 September 2008. 'Truth be told I never had any financial gains from you. All the films you cast me in, you have thrown me out after casting me in more, I still am thankful to you.'

Manoj was cast for the character of Satya in *Satya*, but it was changed later. He didn't have any option then, so he had to accept Bhiku Mhatre. It's a different thing that Bhiku Mhtare turned out to be a game changer. As an actor, it must have been very disrespectful for Manoj to be thrown out of films, but Ramu probably crossed his limits when he offered Sambha's role to Manoj in his ambitious film *Ram Gopal Varma ki Aag*.

In a *Times of India* report published in August 2006, Ram Kamal Mukherjee wrote, 'As per our sources, Ramu offered Sambha's role to Manoj. They have talked about the role till 2:30 in the night, but they did not agree on many points, and they decided not to work with each other ever again. They couldn't resolve their personal matters.'

Manoj also made things clear in an interview given to DNA on 22 September 2006. He was asked why he refused to work in *Ram Gopal Varma Ki Aag*. 'He offered me Sambha's role. We can't see eye to eye.'

Why?

'You can't make a newspaper some courtroom drama. It was wise to go separate ways after so much disagreement. I have never hidden my praise and problems with anyone.'

In an interview with *Mumbai Mirror* on 2 March 2007, he said: 'Yes, I trusted Ram Gopal Varma because he called me his younger brother. I was an idiot to trust him. I was promised good roles in interesting projects, but I was later replaced by big stars. I trusted him blindly. But I couldn't tolerate insults after a point.' He went even further in an interview with *Bollywood Hungama* on 3 January 2007 and said, 'You won't see me doing films with him any more. The wounds he has given, would never heal.'

But why did Ramu not offer any films to Manoj before *Ram Gopal Varma ki Aag*? His acting capabilities were beyond doubt. If Ramu wanted, he could have made a space for Manoj in any of his films. So, was there anything else in between *Road* and *Aag* that started problems?

While talking to many people around Manoj, I realized that there was probably one more story about this animosity. This story goes back to 2000, when the preparations for the release of *Dil Pe Mat Le Yaar!* were going on. Manoj was having dinner with Shabana and Prabal Pandey, Manoj's friend, at a Chinese restaurant in Four Bungalows area. One of Shabana's friends, who worked at Ramu's Factory, also came. He knew Shabana from her Delhi days. He said something during dinner that Manoj didn't like. Manoj got angry and confronted that guy. The person came out of the restaurant and called up Ramu and threatened to file an FIR against Manoj. Ramu helped him. This didn't go down well with Manoj, who thought the reason behind his anger was justified. Neither Ramu nor Manoj said anything about this in the media, but some unconfirmed reports were in the media. Shabana, in an interview with Rediff in 2008, said, 'How can I be the reason? I think, only Ram Gopal Varma or Manoj Bajpayee can answer this question.'

Unfortunately, Manoj had an argument with Hansal on the same day. Manoj was not happy with one of Hansal's interviews. One of Manoj's friends told me that Hansal had praised Saurabh Shukla in the interview and overlooked Manoj to some extent.

After the incident at the Chinese restaurant, Ramu finished his projects with Manoj, but didn't cast him again, or threw him out after casting him. *Aag* added fuel to the fire. Probably, Ramu was in no mood to let go of things easily. He started a blog war. He wrote a post titled 'Stars and Actors' and compared Shah Rukh and Manoj. He wrote: 'At an Awards function post *Satya* release when Manoj Bajpayee came on stage people were screaming out Bhikku Bhai despite Shah Rukh's presence, which obviously thrilled Manoj. I cautioned Manoj after the event not to get carried away as he should realize that they are calling him by his character's name and not his personal name. Shah Rukh by that time might have given 25 super hits but nobody remembers what his character's name was in any of those films. That is the power of a star. Actors die along with their characters and stars live on.'[49]

This blog is not available on the internet now, but one of Ramu's fans had made a mirror blog and it can be found there.

Manoj also wrote a blog post on 11 September 2008. 'I have been attached to him (Ramu). After watching me in *Bandit*

Queen and *Tamanna*, he offered me *Satya* and a small role in *Daud*, after that. We have had a good professional relationship. However, I won't be able to comment much on the creative aspects, since it was mostly Anurag Kashyap or Saurabh Shukla I interacted with.'[50]

He added, 'Mr Ram Gopal Varma, on his blog said that when in award ceremonies, people called me Bhiku Mhatre (my character's name in *Satya*), I used to get excited as they called me and not the other stars. This has been the only reason of tension between us. He has spent his entire life on false beliefs.

'I was happy with the success of *Satya* and was happy that I got noticed. I was happy that I had an abode. Hence, despite all the prevailing apprehensions between us, I was thankful to him. A passion to become an actor drove me to Mumbai. I had dreams to become successful and lead a good life with my family. I never wanted to compete, and I think that I achieved more than I had ever dreamt of.

'The problem with Ram Gopal Varma has been that he always wanted Manoj as an actor who can flatter him all the time. He wanted someone who has no self-respect. I just want to say that please Mr Varma stop maligning my character. Our creative and professional ventures are over now. And there's no question of an emotional attachment because it never existed at first hand. So, Mr Varma, if you feel too much for me, you better keep my photograph and look at it every morning. But stop faking.'

He concluded, 'However, I know that you wouldn't leave me; else your own existence would be in danger. All I want to say is that no one expected *Satya*'s success. We did what we could to the best of our abilities. As an actor, I performed my best and as a director you did what you thought was the best.

'No one owes anything to each other now, but I'm still grateful to you. However, you should learn to respect my feelings and emotions too. But who am I saying all this to? To a person who doesn't believe in any form of relationship, may it be that of a husband and a wife or that of a brother and a sister, or any other form of emotional bond, for that matter.

'For the last nine years I have been trying to make things work out between us. Professionally, there was never much of an economic gain from you. And you denied me the role after casting than you ever gave me roles, but I'm still thankful for what I got from you. May God bless you and keep you happy.

'I always wanted to share this with you people. There's more to all this, which is likely to come up if Mr Varma refuses to mend his ways. I respect him, but that doesn't mean I'm a menial worker who would do whatever he asks for.'

Since I typed the post for Manoj, I asked him if it's fine to write such strong language. He said yes because this is how he feels. The cold war continued even after this blog. Ram Gopal Varma wrote a blog in 2010, in which he described an incident involving Basu Chatterjee.[51]

'I was at my office in Mumbai when my receptionist called me and said someone called Basu Chatterjee was there to meet me. When I asked the receptionist who he is, he said, "He claims that he is a director." I got a shock, and I was wondering why he came to my office. In fact, I didn't even know how he looks like as I never saw a picture of his. I walked to the reception to see a gentle-looking elderly man and I welcomed him into my room.

'Even as I was wondering why he came to meet me I offered him coffee and started telling him how I used to stand in line outside Ramkrishna theatre in Hyderabad to watch his films. He was very pleased and told me that he knew it as I acknowledged that fact many a time in my interviews over the years.

'After a chat finally he told me why he came to meet me. Apparently, he has a script and a producer, but he does not have access to any actors. He was desperately trying to get in touch with Manoj Bajpayee but was unable to do so. So, he came to me to seek my help in accessing Manoj.

'I said "Sure" and I went into the other room and called Manoj. His phone was off and so I called his secretary. The secretary told me Manoj was out of town and when I asked him if they knew that Basu Chatterjee was trying to get in touch he said "Yeah, I am figuring out how to get rid of him".

'I was pretty taken aback with those words, but knowing Manoj, I knew these words of his secretary could not be of Manoj, but the general drift was very clear to me that Manoj for whatever reasons was not interested in working with Basu Chatterjee.

'Then I came in and told Basuji "Manoj is not in town, so I will talk to him and get back." He chatted for some more time and left.

'Then a few days later Basuji called me on phone and said "Apparently Manoj is back in town but I have this feeling that he doesn't want to work with me." I didn't know what to say to that.'

Like other fights, time healed this separation between Ramu and Manoj as well. Ramu also walked the talk and sent praiseworthy SMSs to Manoj after his award-winning performances. They decided to patch up by 2012. As per a report in NDTV.com. Manoj said, 'We patched up. I am no more the angry Manoj Bajpayee that I used to be. I am grateful to Ramu for making my career. He had belief in me. We did have issues with each other, but they have now been sorted. Ramu even messages me when he sees my films or promos. We compliment each other.'[52]

Then it became public. Manoj went to Ramu's office to watch the promo of *Satya 2*. Then on 1 November 2016, Ramu praised Manoj's work in Neeraj Pandey's short film *Ouch* in a tweet.[53]

After a few days, Manoj was seen doing a small role in Ramu's *Sarkar 3*.

Feud with Anurag

Anurag Kashyap was barely twenty-two years old when he arrived in Mumbai. However, his talent was put on the right path by Manoj Bajpayee. When Anurag first met Manoj in Mumbai, he was writing a film called *Nagrajan*, to be directed by Kamal Swaroop. Manoj was not getting good roles even after *Bandit*

Queen. 'I had seen his play *Netua* and *Bandit Queen*,' says Anurag. 'I asked him to work in *Nagrajan* and arranged a meeting with Kamal Swaroop. I showed faith in him, and he liked this gesture so much that wherever he went for work he took me along. When Manoj bhai got *Tamanna*, he made me meet Mahesh and Mukesh Bhatt. I started working there. Similarly, he made me meet Ramu. He became like an elder brother.'

Manoj and Anurag could be found together for most of the time during the shooting of *Satya*. They had food together in Manoj's Shashtri Nagar house. They shared an informal relationship, but Anurag had to pay the price for it when Manoj was ready to hit him with a brick. 'We made fun of Manoj bhai's English,' says Anurag. 'His face twitched when he spoke English. One evening I teased him, and he got so angry outside Gulzar's house that he picked up a stone to beat me up. Hansal Mehta was also there.'

Many stories of those times convey Manoj's short-tempered nature. Anubhav Sinha also shared an anecdote: 'All the friends had come for my wedding. When I was leaving in the car with my wife, I saw Manoj taking a leak in the roadside while Tigmanshu was standing behind him saying something. When the driver started moving, all I saw was Manoj chasing Tigmanshu with a brick in hand.'

Vineet Kumar completed the story. 'They fought physically that day. They didn't talk for many days after that.'

It's apparent that Manoj is a sensitive person and sometimes tends to cross the boundary in a sentimental state. Anurag had seen him from close quarters and worked enough with him to understand the occasional drift. Anurag had written *Shool* based on Manoj's idea. He had written it with Benares as the backdrop and was supposed to direct it also. But he dragged his feet after creative differences with Ram Gopal Varma, though he wrote as per Ramu's will under Manoj's pressure. He also actively took part in casting and many other departments. Whether it was insecurity induced due to Anurag's amazing talent or something else, Ramu probably didn't give Anurag his fair share of credit for *Shool*. 'Whatever I learnt, I learnt it from Ramu sir,' says Anurag. 'He is my teacher in the film industry. But when we had an argument, he would say, "What will you do, go to media?" This broke my heart. I decided not to work with him. I will do everything else like drinking, eating etc., but I will not work with him.'

After coming out of the Ramu camp, Anurag worked on films like *Water* (2005) and *Mission Kashmir* (2000), but he had to leave these projects for various reasons. In such a mental state, he made his short film titled *Last Train to Mahakali*. Anurag told me that he had finished writing *Mirage* by then. 'Sudhir Mishra wanted to produce the film and he asked me if I would be able to make the film with a Rs 50-lakh budget. I wanted to make the film with Manoj and Raveena. When I told Manoj about it, he said he wouldn't charge lesser than Raveena. It was not possible to give him Rs 17 lakh as per the film's budget. He was not ready to work for a lesser amount. I was upset because when I didn't want to do *Shool*, he pressurized me to do it. Then I had an argument with Ramu because I didn't get the credit. Whatever little credit I got for *Shool* was due to the director Eeshwar Nivas. After this, I decided to make films only with newcomers.'

Manoj's rejection of Anurag's film shook the base of their relationship. Anurag probably saw it as deception on Manoj's part. Or maybe Anurag was in a hurry to encash the opportunity.

Manoj, in an interview, said, 'I don't know why but Anurag felt I am not showing enough interest in his first project as a director. We stopped talking. I also didn't try to address rumours or bridge the gap. We both were young and full of ego then. We didn't talk to each other for years and stopped any sort of communication.'[54]

Two talented people in the same industry didn't communicate for ten years. But when Manoj was going through a rough patch, he called up Anurag after watching *Dev.D* in February–March 2009. 'I watched good films at home those days,' says Manoj. 'I remembered how Anupam Kher said that he asks for work from directors even after being so successful. I said it's a good thing. I called up Dibakar Banerjee after watching *Oye Lucky! Lucky Oye!* (2008). Called up Neeraj Pandey after watching *A Wednesday* (2008). Neeraj called me for a meeting. During that bad time, he said he is a fan of mine and that he wants to work with me, but I will have to wait a little. I am writing something. I saw *Dev.D*. I was in a dilemma whether I should call Anurag up or not. I decided I would call him but would not ask for work. I called him and said that his film was good, and he should keep working like this. I disconnected the call after wishing him luck.'

This call broke the ice to some extent. By 2009, Anurag was out of his struggle period. He had already carved out a niche for himself as an able director and had matured as a person. When he started writing *Gangs pf Wasseypur*, the first name he had in mind was of Manoj Bajpayee. 'I received a call from Anurag at around 10.30 in the night after nearly two years,' says Manoj. 'I was about to go to bed. The voice said: "Bhai, Anurag speaking this side. Would you read a script and work with me?" I thought he had gone mad. "What's the script?" I asked him. He said, "Let's meet tomorrow or the day after whenever you have the time." I asked where he was then. When he said he was in the office, I asked for his address. He asked whether I was coming because it's too late. I said yes. Just keep a bottle of white wine handy. Then Anurag wondered if I had stopped drinking Bacardi! I told him I had ditched it a long time ago. Then he asked me to come and said he would narrate the script. I went, we hugged and then he gave me a narration till 12.30 in the night. We discussed the film. I told him I would read the script and asked him to get a drink. He drank his whiskey, and I had my wine. We hugged and left for home.'

During the narration, Manoj suggested Sardar Khan as his character's name and Anurag agreed. *Gangs of Wasseypur* ended the cold war between them. It became a hit and made Anurag a favourite with the bigger studios. Earlier, his films were critically acclaimed but were not known for doing big business. *Gangs of Wasseypur* ended his stint as a small-budget director.

However, while researching for this book, I kept wondering whether it's mandatory for creative people to be headstrong. Manoj, in an interview, said, 'Anurag is gullible. He would believe if someone filled his ears that Manoj has said something about you. And I was also infamous in the industry for my anger.'[55]

'I know all of Manoj's group from back then,' saya Harsh Chhaya. 'They all had come for success. They all have terrific aggression. I had witnessed people from the same group not talking to each other and then patching up. This was normal.'

Manoj and Anurag have a changed equation now, and Manoj keeps praising the latter. I remember Manoj calling me up in the night and dictating a blog post after a controversy about Anurag and his choice of films.

The title for the blog post was 'Be friends with Anurag Kashyap, don't judge him'. It read, 'Why do we expect Anurag Kashyap to change society? You should congratulate him if he is writing a new cinematic language. Have a cup of tea with him and head home. A film on Dalits can't be made, a film can be made on a good story, and Dalits can be at the centre of that story. Their social positioning can be there. A story is desperately needed for a film. Cinema doesn't change society. I have been saying this for years. If it could, Shyam Benegal and Govind Nihalani could have changed society. The Indian film industry hasn't seen a superstar like Amitabh Bachchan, who always led the downtrodden on the silver screen. So, why did the situation not change? Why can't the conversation about the changing language of cinema happen with Anurag? Has anyone asked him how he makes films of his liking in this commercial market? Has anyone asked him what he sacrificed in his journey? Do you even know why he couldn't release some of his films? Do you know how terribly he fared till the release of *Black Friday*? He has also become a passionate filmmaker in his pursuit of remaining true to his craft, don't instigate him.'[56]

With this blog post, Manoj put an end to all the speculations about his fight with Anurag Kashyap. The two were back and how!

Chapter 20

The Comeback

'In many ways, the National Awards have lost their charm even more than the private awards. These are also prone to politics, regionalism and nepotism.'

The second decade of the new millennium turned out to be a good one for Manoj Bajpayee. He had reached a stage where he didn't have to prove anything to anyone. He learnt the right balance between commercial and off-beat films, the projects which could give him satisfaction as an actor. He found a way to not lose the right essence of his goals in the pursuit of commercial success. Films like *Gali Guleiyan*, *Aligarh* and *Bhonsle* brought out his latent potential and what he is capable of.

Manoj Bajpayee has a special connection with Amitabh Bachchan. If it was *Zanjeer* that inspired him to take up acting as career, it was *Aks* that gave him a chance to witness the legend from close quarters. Prakash Jha brought the two actors back together in the 2011 film *Aarakshan*. In the film when Manoj compared Amitabh Bachchan with zero in a hit dialogue, his fans whistled and applauded. He worked with Saif Ali Khan for the second time after *LOC* in *Aarakshan*. It was a commercially successful film which made Manoj a part of the Jha camp. However, it didn't initiate any friendship off-screen between them. Manoj says,

'I have an ideal working relationship with Prakash Jha. Though I don't talk to him over the phone. I really respect him as a senior.'

Prakash Jha reciprocated similar sentiments. 'Manoj is from theatre. He has many references from real life in his subconscious, which he uses during acting. For example, he is different in *Bhonsle* or *The Family Man* or *Raajneeti*. It's his hunger as an artist that inspires him to prepare and fine-tune every character differently. I don't have any special tuning with Manoj, I enjoy working with him because he understands the nuances.'

Lanka, which was produced by Vikram Bhatt and directed by Maqbool Khan, also released in 2011. It was previously titled *Vibishan*, but the name was changed after a long discussion between Manoj and Vikram. The film was shot in UP's Bijnor. The year turned out to be happier for Manoj when Shabana gave birth to a daughter in February 2011.

Manoj wrote on his blog, 'I need blessings from all of you. No, not for me! I need blessings for my daughter. She is born on 23rd February. This is the most memorable day for me and my wife. First time, I am getting the happiness of fatherhood and also the feeling of responsibility. First time, I am getting emotional about how life will take a turn. Is my daughter born in a reformed and ideal world or many reformations are still pending? And answers come which all parents must have given that world can never be an ideal place.'[57]

The daughter was named Ava Nayla. 'Ava means bird and Nayla means a great start. I picked both names. Shabana liked the names so much we started calling our daughter Ava Nayla.'

The year 2012, in a way, was a game changer in modern Bollywood film-making. Many directors experimented with style and substance, and Anurag Kashyap was the frontrunner among them. His *Gangs of Wasseypur* wrote a new chapter for rowdy-gangster movies in Hindi. Manoj lost weight for this role, he also changed his look and demeanour to a great extent to play a cheap, conniving, highly motivated and dangerous gangster,

Sardar Khan. He became the backbone of the two-part film, which received a long-standing ovation at prestigious film events including Cannes. The nearly bald look in the film wasn't part of the script. Manoj was suffering from hair loss at that time. Some adjustments had to be made to the story to justify the bald look.

Gangs of Wasseypur released on 22 June 2012. Many critics include this film as one of the top 100 Hindi films ever made. The *Hollywood Reporter* wrote, '*Gangs of Wasseypur* puts Tarantino in a corner with its cool command of cinematically-inspired and referenced violence, ironic characters and breathless pace.'[58]

Whatever reputation was harmed due to some bad films in the previous decade, Manoj covered up with this one performance. The *Indian Express* wrote, 'This is Bajpayee's best and even better performance than *Satya*.'[59]

Anupama Chopra wrote in the *Hindustan Times*, 'This is undoubtedly Bajpayee's best performance since Bhiku Mhatre in *Satya*. Sardar Khan has an insatiable appetite for sex and power. He murders with glee. And yet he's charming.'[60]

This was also the film which made Manoj meet his fanboy Pankaj Tripathi.

The year 2012 also saw the release of *Chittagong* and *Chakravyuh*. Directed by Bedabrata Pain, Manoj considers his role in *Chittagong* as one of his best, but the film didn't work at the box office. It also suffered due to the lack of advertising. Manoj's guru, Barry John, had also played a character—Magistrate Wilkinson—in the film.

A major part of *Chittagong* was shot at the Gorumara National Park near Bhutan. Manoj didn't like the behaviour of an assistant director during the shoot. Nawazuddin Siddiqui, his co-actor in the film, narrated a funny incident. 'That assistant thought highly of himself. Everyone, except Manoj bhai, was new. His way of calling us for the shot was also not good. Manoj bhai was observing all this. One day, when I discussed it with him, he said, "Let me do something about it." He called his personal assistant and got half a sleeping pill mixed in that assistant director's tea. That guy, who use to speak loudly, got a bit relaxed in no time. The shooting was happening at night. After a while, he was completely asleep. Everybody thought he was unconscious. Some of the girls said he became unconscious after eating too many fritters. We had a good laugh about it later. Manoj is one of the funniest people I have met.'

Manoj played a Naxal leader in Prakash Jha's *Chakravyuh*. Manoj's performance in *Chakravyuh* was praised despite the film not working commercially. Rohit Khilnani wrote in *India Today*, 'Manoj Bajpayee as Rajan is perfect and convincing in the role.'[61]

The year 2013 saw Manoj collaborating with Neeraj Pandey in *Special 26*. While Akshay Kumar played a thug called Ajay Singh, Manoj was seen as a CBI officer Waseem Khan in the film. Neeraj wanted to work with Manoj for a long time, and he had promised a collaboration during Manoj's tough days, so it was a special bond for both. It was a hit.

Sanjay Gupta's *Shootout at Wadala* and Prakash Jha's *Satyagraha*, both big-budget projects, released in the same year. Manoj and Sanjay had earlier worked together in *Dus Kahaniyaan* and *Acid Factory*. The film did average business, but Manoj was in his groove. His dialogues became an instant hit.

Satyagraha, which was inspired by Anna Hazare's movement, had a huge starcast: Amitabh Bachchan, Manoj Bajpayee, Ajay Devgn, Kareena Kapoor and Arjun Rampal. Manoj played a negative role. The film tanked badly. It was a huge jolt for Prakash Jha.

Manoj voiced the character of Yudhisthir in an animation film, *Mahabharat* in 2013. He was seen in just one film *Anjaan*, that too in Tamil, in 2014.

The next year also saw him in just one film—the Boney Kapoor production *Tevar*. Shubhra Gupta wrote in the *Financial Express*, 'It is Manoj Bajpayee who brings "asli dum" to this utterly predictable, loud, done-to-death "Violent Love Story". He's done all of this before—the leering, the jeering, the dialogue delivery—

but he does it with full zest. I wouldn't like to meet his character coming down a dark street.'[62]

The film didn't work at the box office, but it brought more repercussions for Arjun Kapoor than Manoj Bajpayee.

Aligarh, directed by Hansal Mehta, released in 2016. Undoubtedly one of the finest, if not the finest, films of Manoj's career, *Aligarh* saw the layered story of a homosexual professor Dr Shrinivas Ramchandra Siras of Aligarh Muslim University. Manoj brought out the pain and harassment faced by the lonely professor in such a way that everyone questioned the social boundaries they face every day.

Manoj and Hansal worked together many years after *Dil Pe Mat Le Yaar!*. Their conflict lasted for close to fifteen years. Hansal hadn't directly contacted Manoj for the role of Professor Siras. It was suggested by the casting director Mukesh Chhabra. 'The best thing about Manoj is that he can't be typecast. You would never know how he is going to perform. You can mimic all the actors in the industry but not Manoj,' says Mukesh Chhabra.

Manoj also worked with his close friend Ashish Vidyarthi, who played his lawyer, after twenty-two years in *Aligarh*.

Manoj, in a way, also showed his gratitude to Barry John, through *Aligarh*. A screening before the film's release was arranged. 'He [Barry John] hugged me after the film. He had tears in his eyes, and he didn't say anything for ten minutes. His voice was choked with emotion.'

When I asked Barry about it, he said, 'Yes, this is true. It was a character study for Manoj. Such realistic portrayal in Hindi cinema is rare. I hadn't seen such a complete and mature performance by Manoj till date. He was mentally and physically the character he was playing, and his acting was mesmerizing. He was so naïve, introvert and pure as Siras that all the people blaming him looked like monsters.'

Barry wrote a letter to Manoj after watching *Aligarh*, which Manoj has kept as an award. No other Hindi film treated 'gays' with so much sensibility and empathy before *Aligarh*. It was mostly seen as a funny theme. This film, despite being about a lonely professor, never for a second, presented gays as aliens or weak people.

Barry himself is a part of the marginalized community and the film probably brought out the pain and indifference he had been facing all his life. One of his group members told me, 'Years ago, some people had put vulgar pamphlets on the seats of Kamani Auditorium that talked about Barry John's sexual identity. It was a shocking thing for the group then. When we asked, he confirmed it.'

Hansal-Manoj and the entire team gave a creative reply to people opposing the homosexual community. Manoj personally might not have been a part of the community, but he had close ties with the community, which enabled him to find answers for his queries and gave him a new perspective. Manoj had spent a long time with Barry, and he respected the boundary between the personal and professional.

One major reason behind *Aligarh's* realistic portrayal was its very sensible team. Apurva Asrani, the film's writer, has never hidden his sexuality. The film's transgender cinematographer Satya Rai Nagpaul and costume designer Piya Benegal were a part of the LGBTQ+ community and saw everything from a fresh perspective.

Apurva was the one who took Manoj to a gay club in Mumbai's outskirts before the release of *Satya*. He interviewed Manoj for the *Hindustan Times* in December 2019. 'Even back in the day, I remember, it was easy for me to confide in him. Once, before *Satya* released, I took Manoj to a gay party in suburban Mumbai. He was quite a hit with the boys and blushed when they flirted with him. When we left, he had a huge grin on his face, and jokingly reminded me that he was still straight; that the party hadn't converted him.'

Manoj, in the same interview, said, 'I remember that party. You know why I was so comfortable? Because my teacher was Barry John, who had come out to me before I even knew what the word gay meant. I stayed in his house, slept in his bed even, but he was dignified and gracious. And after I got to know you as well, I knew that I could never pigeonhole gay men into stereotypes.'

Probably this is the reason he could play Professor Siras with so much innocence, something that could only be felt, not understood or studied. Remember the scene from *Aligarh* where Manoj sees two men dancing like anything at a party after winning the case in the court? The way he blushes is a testimony of how close he was to the character. It was beyond acting.

Much of *Aligarh*'s shooting took place in Bareilly, because the Bareilly College building resembled the Aligarh Muslim University's building. A local journalist, Dr Rajesh Sharma had worked as the line producer during the Bareilly schedule. He was told the unit needs a bungalow with a lawn to shoot a party scene. He immediately arranged his friend Rajat Khandelwal's bungalow for the scene. Dr Sharma told me, 'I suddenly discovered that the lawn is required for a gay party scene. I was worried how Rajat, the owner, would feel about it. Bareilly is a small town, and anything can turn up the heat here. I told Rajat the entire thing, and thankfully he didn't object to it. The real hurdle came after it. Next day, when the shooting started, Payal, a member of Hansal's team, came to me and said, "Sir, will you be able to find a man who is also a classical dancer?" I asked why. She said "The person we had called couldn't perform as per the director's will." As per the script, they needed somebody who looked dignified and was gay as per the role. Finally, I had to play that character. I took permission from my wife for the role. I was sent to the vanity van and I came out as "gay". The scene was shot in the presence of 300 people and was finalized in just one take. Manoj Bajpayee came forward and hugged me.'

Aligarh is pathbreaking in many senses. It's a masterclass in acting. Consider the scene in which Manoj is listening to Lata Mangeshkar's '*Aapki nazron ne samjha*' in a dark, closed room. He is not acting for the camera. He is simply enjoying his drink and repeating the song in his feeble voice. All he does is some hand gestures, but it's so powerful that it remains with the viewers for a long, long time, maybe forever. It's a classic film, because it's not a constructed reality, it's something that comes naturally to all of us. For the character, Manoj took classes in Marathi diction, read Marathi poetry and understood the finesse of the language and its dialect. It was only Professor Siras on screen! Manoj, in an interview, said that Dr Siras's way of speaking was inspired from the director of *Missing*—Mukul Abhyankar.[63]

Rajkummar Rao played a journalist in *Aligarh*. For him, it was a process to see Manoj prepare for his role. Rajkummar said in an interview, 'Working with him was wonderful. Acting is about reacting to the other person. Manoj sir creates such magical moments onscreen that it feels amazing working with him.'[64]

The critics were blown by Manoj's performance in the film. Shweta Kaushal wrote in the *Hindustan Times*, 'Storytelling aside, *Aligarh* is supported by the immense acting prowess of Manoj Bajpayee. Be it the body language, the hint of a Marathi accent or the poetic mind of a professor, Manoj pays attention to the smallest of details. We've seen him as Bhiku Mhatre (*Satya*) and Sardar Khan (*Gangs of Wasseypur*), but Siras is by far his career best. A spell-binding performance with the trappings of warmth, love and agony, it is hard to look away from him.'[65]

Manoj received the Filmfare Best Actor (Critics) for *Aligarh* in 2017 but lost out to Akshay Kumar for *Rustom* (2016) at the National Film Awards. Renowned filmmaker Priyadarshan was the head of the jury for the National Awards that year. It must have been heartbreaking for Manoj. 'At the time of *Shool*, the jury was divided between me and Mohanlal. In the end, the award went to Mohanlal for *Vanprastham* for a couple of votes. I didn't feel bad at all, because it went to a person I was a huge fan of for that role.'

Look at the paradox: *Aligarh* couldn't even make a place for itself in the eighty-nine films watched by the jury. Now, based on his bad experiences, Manoj doesn't have many expectations from the National Awards. 'In many ways, the National Awards have lost their charm even more than the private awards. These are also prone to politics, regionalism and nepotism.'

It was a pleasant coincidence that Manoj received the National Award for *Bhonsle* after a few months of this conversation. It was another exceptional performance from Manoj, and it must have taken away some of the pain associated with his bad experiences at the National Awards.

Awards or no awards, *Aligarh* presented a totally different Manoj Bajpayee, one who set a new benchmark for all sorts of acting, be it films or theatre. From Barry John to Naseeruddin Shah to Gajraj Rao to Piyush Mishra, everyone believed it was a milestone in Hindi cinema acting.

However, Shabana's reaction to *Aligarh* was very different. It, in fact, frightened Manoj and Hansal. Hansal invited Manoj to see the film after the final edit. Manoj called Shabana there after watching the film and sat with Hansal outside the studio. Shabana, after watching the film, came out and walked down the stairs, took an auto and went home. Hansal thought she didn't like the film, but she had liked it so much she couldn't control her tears and that's why she went home. I remember asking Barry about Manoj's range. 'Manoj is getting better and mature. I think his best is yet to come. His hunger for challenges is still there,' was his reply.

In 2016, Manoj was seen in three other lead roles—*Traffic*, *Budhia Singh: Born to Run* and *Saat Uchakkey*. It was a very crucial year for his career. He played the coach of Odisha's child prodigy Budhia Singh. This role is very close to his heart. Rohit Vats wrote in the *Hindustan Times*, 'Bajpayee's Das is bursting with energy and is ready to take on the world. He knows the art of media manipulation and is subtle in approach. He has walked a tight rope here as a slight mistake would have made him the villain of this story.'[66]

Unfortunately, the film didn't work.

In *Traffic*, he played a traffic inspector who stops a fast-moving city like Mumbai for a noble cause. It was the remake of a Malayalam film. Its moderate business boosted Manoj's confidence as the film was totally banking on his shoulders. He had done everything to publicize the film. Something interesting happened during the publicity campaign of *Traffic*. Shah Rukh Khan also reached the spot where Manoj was talking to the press. Shah Rukh said, 'We have worked together in theatre since childhood. I have learnt a lot from Manoj. We have done a lot of fun things together. I am really proud of him. I recently watched *Aligarh* and liked it a lot. '

Saat Uchakkey was a comedy film with actors such as Manoj Bajpayee, Kay Kay Menon, Anupam Kher, Aparshakti Khurana, Vijay Raaz and Annu Kapoor playing pivotal roles. Directed by Sanjeev Sharma, commercial success remained elusive for this one.

Manoj was seen in three films in 2017: *Naam Shabana*, *Sarkar 3* and *Rukh*. He didn't have a sizeable role in any of these, but all of them were important for the narrative. *Naam Shabana* was a film from Neeraj Pandey's repertoire, and a prequel to *Baby* (2015). Taapsee Pannu was in the lead role and Akshay Kumar was in the guest role. The ticket window didn't favour the film.

Sarkar 3 reinstated his friendship with Ramu. Also, Manoj, once again, worked with Amitabh Bachchan.

He probably did *Rukh* for the sake of maintaining a relationship with the makers of the film.

He was seen in many big projects in 2018. Neeraj Pandey's *Aiyaary* saw him in the lead role with Sidharth Malhotra. The lacklustre script doomed the project, but as always, Manoj received appreciation for his role. He did *Baaghi 2* (2018) for his friend Ahmed Khan. They were friends since Ahmed choreographed the song sequence '*Sapne me milti hai*' for *Satya*. With Tiger Shroff in the lead, Manoj played the antagonist, a corrupt police officer, in this blockbuster. Naturally, he was one of the beneficiaries of the hit film.

Then came *Missing* (2018), produced by Manoj Bajpayee and directed by Mukul Abhyankar. It turned out to be a big flop. He worked with old friend Tabu in this psychological thriller.

The actor in Manoj Bajpayee got back on track with *Gali Guleiyan* in the same year. Directed by Dipesh Jain, it is one of those films that would remind Manoj's fans of his acting prowess long after he quits acting. It was a role that took a toll on his mental well-being. 'It was a very intense character. I told the director to finish it quickly on the eighteenth day of the shoot as it was taking a toll on me.'

Shabana has also talked about the impact of this role on Manoj at one place. She said Manoj could be seen talking to himself during the film. Ranvir Shorey played Manoj's friend Ganeshi in *Gali Guleiyan*. 'I did the film only because Manoj was doing the lead role,' says Ranvir.

Manoj's old friend and theatre director Robin Das has also played a small role in the film.

Milap Milan Zaveri's *Satyameva Jayate* hit the screens on 15 August 2018. John Abraham and Manoj Bajpayee were in the central roles. Akshay Kumar's *Gold* (2018) was also released the same day. *Satyameva Jayate* not only held the fort but also garnered enough money to be declared a superhit. Nobody doubted Manoj's acting abilities, but such films gave big ticket producers the confidence to bankroll Manoj for commercially crucial projects.

Love Sonia (2018) and *Bhonsle* hit the festival circuit and reached selected audiences in 2018 itself. Manoj didn't want to do

Love Sonia. 'I have played a pimp in the film. I wasn't interested in the role. It was very upsetting for me; I didn't want to do the film. But David Womark (one of the makers of *Life of Pi* [2012]) was after my life. I think all American producers are expert at negotiating with actors. He somehow managed to convince me. Though I didn't like the character, I am happy to be a part of this film.'

Manoj was back to playing dacoit Maan Singh in Abhishek Chaubey's *Sonchiriya* (2019). Though Sushant Singh Rajput was in the lead role, he completely understood the situation and the stalwarts he was working with. Sushant, on the very first day, touched Manoj's feet and asked for his blessings. Such an emotional gesture by a young star instilled respect for Sushant in everyone's heart. Ranvir Shorey, who has also played an important role in the film, told me, 'It was probably Manoj Bhai's first shot in the film in which a few arms dealers come to meet him beside a pond. Manoj, upon seeing the place, says, "It seems I have come here before." Later, we got to know he gave his first shot for *Bandit Queen* near that pond.'

But Manoj's real and biggest achievement in 2019 was the web series *The Family Man*. It isn't that he wasn't offered a web series before, but he was waiting for something unique to come his way. Needless to say, *The Family Man* made Manoj a star among youngsters, a place even commercial megastars crave for.

The character of Shrikant Tiwari has a special place in Manoj's heart. 'I have made the most number of notes among all my characters for this one. I ran to my notebook whenever I remembered a small detail. This is the only work I did for eight months. But Shabana was not happy with me working on OTT. I convinced her how it was different. She questioned if it was about money, and why do I need to jeopardize my career, I will finish everything. I asked her, "How did *Narcos* become so popular?" She was of the opinion that ultimately it's a serial. She probably didn't realize the strength of OTT till she watched the first season.'

The year 2020 witnessed the Covid-19 onslaught. Even Manoj was trapped at a resort in Uttarakhand for more than two months with his family. He was seen during the lockdown in a Netflix film titled *Mrs Serial Killer* (2020). It was such a small role that when I asked him for an interview regarding the role, he refused. However, he lent his voice for one of my poems during the Covid-19 period and it became viral in no time.

Vichitra sa ye waqt hai
anisht ka sanchar hai
kaal ke kapaal par
jwaar ka ek bhaar hai
ghar raha to jeet tay
veerta main haar hai
adrishya ye shatru hai
vikat kintu auzaar hai
bhor ki prateeksha main
raat ab bezaar hai
sachet rahe to jeet tay
veerta main haar hai
sparsh se shool chubhe
pyaar main bhi haar hai
ye kaun sa daur hai
har aur hi sanhaar hai
chintit raha to jeet tay
uchshrinhla hua to haar hai
ghar raha to jeet tay
veerta main haar hai

Bhonsle benefitted due to the high demand of content on OTTs. It reached the viewers in search of quality content. From *Satya* to *Aligarh* to *Bhonsle*, Manoj has portrayed different dimensions of a Marathi persona. Directed by Devashish Makhija, the film touched the issue of discrimination against north Indians in Mumbai, something which is very close to Manoj's heart as well. It is noteworthy that in 2008, Manoj was targeted by the Shiv Sena for speaking out on the issue of north Indians. He had to issue a clarification then.

Devashish and Manoj had worked together in a short film *Tandav* earlier. It was Manoj's way of assessing Devashish's talent. He got the Filmfare Best Actor (Short Film) for *Tandav*.

Manoj has done other short films too including Shirish Kunder's *Kriti* (2016) and Neeraj Pandey's *Ouch* (2016).

In the end of 2020 when nobody was sure of watching films in a theatre, *Suraj Pe Mangal Bhari* hit the screens. It was bound to nosedive.

The duration between 2011 and 2020 paid Manoj back for his dedication, maturity and discipline. He became more experimental and braver in all formats, and renewed producers' faith in his acting's commercial viabilities. Not only that, he also tried his hand at rapping in Anubhav Sinha's video '*Bihar me ka ba*'.

Manoj, the actor-star, was back to the top, where he belonged and ready to explode.

Chapter 21

An Actor Par Excellence

What does Manoj Bajpayee stand for? Does his journey belong only to him, or does he represent something bigger than what meets the eyes? In short, what exactly is the meaning of being Manoj Bajpayee?

When I asked actor Pankaj Tripathi all these questions, this is what he had to say: 'I was doing theatre in Patna. I watched *Satya* in Patna's Apsara Theatre, with Devendra Raj Ankur. After watching the film, I felt if a person from Belwa can become such an acclaimed actor, so can a person from Belsand. Manoj bhaiyya's success gave me a boost.'

Interestingly, Belwa and Belsand are only 60 km apart, but the two had never met before. Pankaj, like Eklavya, kept learning from a distance. 'We were doing a Vijay Tendulkar play called *Jaati Hi Poocho Sadhu Ki* in Patna. Many boys came and met me to participate in the play, many of them were from Bettiah. Those middle-class boys wanted to act. They were happy that their parents had permitted them to work in theatre. Five boys from Bettiah worked with me in that play and all of them are in Mumbai now,' says Pankaj.

Pankaj believes it was Manoj's success that paved the way for Bihar youngsters in the world of acting. In the twenty-five years of his film career, Manoj has very few commercial hits, but he commands extraordinary respect as an actor. Manoj himself believes it's a miracle that he has survived in this business for so long.

What Manoj means to Pankaj was evident in *The Kapil Sharma Show*, where he almost cried while narrating the incident about Manoj's stolen slippers. I asked Pankaj about such an emotional outburst. 'This is a spiritual connection. I became sentimental thinking how big it was a deal to just meet him at one point in time. I stole his slippers and kept with me, but I am sitting with him today. He also knows me.'

When asked whether the incident happened exactly the way he narrated at the show, he said, 'It was exactly like that. I was kitchen supervisor in Patna's Maurya Hotel. When I got to know Manoj bhaiyya was staying there, I told all the service boys to let me know whenever any order comes from his room so that I can go and deliver. When I told him about my theatre work, he appreciated it. When he left, a service boy told me that he left his slippers. I asked them not to deposit it with the admin. I kept it.'

Not only Pankaj, many other actors also seek inspiration from Manoj. Actor Gulshan Devaiah went to the National Institute of Fashion Technology in Bengaluru in 1997. He watched *Satya* in 1999 and it swept him off the feet. 'All the credit of me being here goes to Ram Gopal Varma and Manoj Bajpayee.'

Manoj comes from a place where electricity reached only in the 1980s. Vishnu Upadhyay, who hails from a nearby village, said, 'Manoj bhaiyya's journey has inspired a whole generation. After watching *Satya*, I had the hope that I could also act. Like him, I also went to Delhi and acted in theatre.'

After working as a journalist, Vishnu is now a film producer.

His impression on colleagues has also been evident, even for established actors like Ravi Kishan who worked with Manoj in *1971* and *Money Hai To Honey Hai*. Ravi Kishan told me, 'He is not insecure. I first met him on the sets of *Aks*. I reached there after much struggle. He met with love and humility. There was a

Bhojpuri connection. Wherever he was shooting, I reached there just to meet the director through him.'

Actor Jaideep Ahlawat, known for films such as *Khatta Meetha* (2010) and *Raazi* (2018), and the web series *Paatal Lok* (2020), in an Instagram chat with Meenakshi Kandwal, said, 'Some people inspire a whole generation, Manoj is one such actor. When *Satya*, *Shool* and *Pinjar* released, a lot of people got inspired then and are getting inspired even now. He witnessed my work in *Chittagong* and suggested my name to Anurag for *Gangs of Wasseypur*. I still remember one of his compliments during *Chittagong*. He came on the sets, met us and told me, "Your eyes are very intense".'

Manoj has become an institution in himself after all these years of struggle and intense preparations. Abhishek Chaubey, who directed him in *Sonchiriya*, *Hungama Hai Kyon Barpa* and *Killer Soup*, said, 'Even after being successful for so many years, he has the hunger of a newcomer. I don't know where it comes from, but every film-maker likes it as this makes their work easier.'

The Family Man showrunners—Raj and DK—talked about Manoj's persona on the sets. 'He can be seen cracking jokes with others on the sets. The director would wonder if he is even prepared, but the first take itself reveals how over-prepared he is.'

Deepesh Jain, the director of *Gali Guleiyan*, says that Bajpayee not only reduced his weight for the role but also cut himself from the world. He talked only with Jain and one of his assistants during the shoot. He kept wearing the same dirty clothes and the make-up prescribed for the character. Nobody could recognize him. 'I joked he is India's answer to Daniel Day-Lewis. He is one of the finest not just in India but in the world.'

Actor Sharib Hashmi, Manoj's wingman in *The Family Man*, shares: 'His discipline is incredible. We might party till 2 a.m., but if the yoga session is scheduled for 5 a.m., it had to start on time. Every day was like a film school with him. There was this table reading for *The Family Man*. We rehearsed afterwards.

But he improvised during the takes. Manoj did everything to make scenes engaging, especially the ones with only information. I was going through a personal crisis during the shoot of *The Family Man*. He helped me in all aspects. Though I didn't need any financial support, he had instructed his staff to remain in touch with me. He is like a friend, philosopher and guide to me.'

While researching about Manoj, it was evident to me that he has a keen interest in promoting young talents. Boishali Sinha, art director of the short film *Tandav*, said, 'He is very focussed. I was working on a project in which Manoj was also expected to join. When the director told him my name, he said it was the right fit for the role. I was surprised he remembered my name and work even after five years.'

Even a star like John Abraham, who has worked with Manoj in *Shootout at Wadala* (2013) and *Satyameva Jayate* (2018), doesn't hold himself back from heaping praises on Manoj. He said in an interview, 'I watch films, but if Manoj Bajpayee is there on the screen, I watch only him. He is an acting institution, and one of the greatest actors in today's Hindi cinema.'[67]

Gajraj Rao echoes the same sentiments. 'I am lucky to have worked with one of the best actors of this subcontinent.'

In the last twenty-five years, Manoj has seen many ups and downs in his acting career. He has walked the razor edge where one mistake can finish anyone's career. Shivam Nair, who has directed films like *Ahista Ahista* (2006), *Maharathi* (2008) and *Naam Shabana* (2017), recalls: 'During *Naam Shabana*, I saw how focused Manoj was. His performance was very balanced which happens when one is rooted. His thoughts have depth, and he explores himself. When people are successful even briefly, the success gets to their head. People lose focus. But my respect for him only grew during the filming of *Naam Shabana*. He is not jealous of anyone. Very few can come out of failure and find themselves again. Manoj has come out of it and has become more spiritual as a person.'

What differentiates Manoj from the others is his undying passion. 'The first thirty years of your life are all about making your dreams come true, and one should leave no stone unturned in achieving what you want.'

Manoj's school friend Nirbhay Tiwari remembers: 'When Manoj was in Delhi, he would sometimes feel nauseous from hunger. Friends like us, from Bihar, used to tell him to focus on his studies. "What will plays get you?" we would ask him. But he was determined. His initial days were marked with so much hardship that anyone else would have called it quits, but he did not. The Almighty supported him and now he is so successful. He hasn't changed even after so much success.'

Manoj is an epitome of grit, self-belief and hard work. A self-made man ready to look in the eye of the storm. A man who has risen against all odds and without any godfather in an industry known for nepotism. He might not be a Rs 100-crore star, but he can give any established actor a run for their money.

Chapter 22

The Journey Continues . . .

Manoj always believed in his dreams. He had a strong desire to make it big as an actor and knew the only way to do that was to step out of his comfort zone, his village. Manoj knew if he could turn his dreams into reality, it would serve as an inspiration to many like him. And that is exactly what happened.

The important question here is: was Manoj able to reach his destination? The answer to that is no. Because the day an artist finds nothing new to attain, they are finished. Besides, Manoj is also on a spiritual journey, the destination of which he is unaware of.

It is safe to say that Manoj is in the golden period of his career, where not only does he have the freedom to experiment with his work but also doesn't have to worry about finances.

In 2021, his web series *The Family Man 2* touched new heights, stamping his presence as the newest star of the OTT space. From my conversations with him during that time, I discerned that Manoj did not particularly like that tag, but he has come around to accepting these labels. Plus he understands the significant freedom these OTTs offer to actors like him. That year, he also starred in films like *Silence: Can You Hear It* and *Dial 100*, which earned him much appreciation.

Manoj did not feature in any notable work in 2022. However, the next year, he starred in three films, with each displaying a distinct shade of him as an actor. *Gulmohar*, which was released on OTT, showed him as a middle-aged man caught in an internal tussle of his family.

Sirf Ek Bandaa Kaafi Hai was a courtroom drama allegedly inspired by the life of Asaram Bapu. Manoj breathed life into the character of advocate P.C. Solanki.

In *Joram*, Manoj took his acting capabilities further. This film is a brilliant example of socially responsible cinema. *Joram* garnered much appreciation and accolades in film festivals worldwide. Not just that, it also received the 2024 Filmfare Award for Best Film (Critics) and Best Story, which is a significant achievement for independent cinema. The Academy of Motion Picture Arts and Sciences Library announced the acquisition of the screenplay of *Joram* for its distinguished Permanent Core Collection.

The *Killer Soup* series was released on OTT towards the end of 2023, where Manoj had a double role.

Manoj has been daringly experimenting with his work, achieving creative satisfaction. His 2024 film *The Fable* is also well on its way to script history. Directed by Ram Reddy, the film premiered at the 2024 Berlin International Film Festival.

Very few Indian actors have managed to showcase such variety in their oeuvre as Manoj Bajpayee. Some never got the opportunity and some couldn't achieve the range Manoj portrayed, despite being talented.

Even after spending close to thirty years in the industry, the amount of effort Manoj puts into preparing for every role is in itself a learning. For him, the third decade of the millennium has been particularly fruitful. However, during this period, he also suffered two personal tragedies. In October 2021, his father, Radhakant Bajpayee, passed away. In December 2022, his mother, Geeta Devi, also passed away. On multiple occasions, Manoj has mentioned that he has never met a man more democratic than his father. The readers have already read in the earlier chapters about the impact his parents have had on his life. No one can fill the void caused by their death. I was also shocked upon receiving this news. I have never met anyone as simple and easy-going as them.

Yes, Manoj has already reached that pinnacle of acting. Though he is graduate by qualification, he is a PhD in acting! And coincidentally, he holds a doctorate from ITM University, Gwalior, which was awarded to him in February 2024.

Acknowledgements

Just as it takes multiple forces of nature to transform a minuscule seed into an imposing, magnificent tree, being able to narrate Manoj Bajpayee's life story is the culmination of the efforts of an army of individuals.

First, immense gratitude to Manoj Bajpayee. One afternoon in October 2019, I suddenly felt the urge to write his biography and called him immediately. I also insisted that he arrange a meeting with his parents and siblings for the sake of the book. He was gracious enough to readily agree. Undoubtedly, this book wouldn't have seen the light of day without his constant support and cooperation.

Apart from Manoj, there are many who helped me bring this book to life. To appreciate them all with a mere thank you would be futile. But then, this act is also important because a single thank you, inscribed on paper, lives on for eternity. So, here goes . . .

It was senior journalist Punya Prasun Bajpai who introduced me to Manoj. In 2008, I had just started a blogging platform and wanted Manoj to write for it. When I casually mentioned this to Punya, he did not waste a second in talking to Manoj and convinced him of the same.

The biggest dilemma I faced after talking to Manoj's family was who to approach next. I wanted to explore the lesser-known facts of his life. I got to know that actor Harsh Chhaya was friends with Manoj. Coincidentally, I had also known Harsh for a long time. When I reached out to him, he was kind enough to not just give me time but also introduce me to Vineet Kumar, who holds a special place in Manoj's life. Thank you to him and Vineet, through whom I went on to meet other people crucial to Manoj's life.

I would also like to extend a heartfelt thanks to Piyush Mishra and Gajraj Rao. Not only did they regale me with many old memories and incidents but also gave me the space to call or message them at any time to arrange calls with other people. This is how I could connect with Anurag Kashyap, Anubhav Sinha, Saurabh Shukla, Pankaj Tripathi, Makarand Deshpande, Vijay Raj, Anil Chaudhary, Anish Ranjan, Nikhil Verma, Prakash Jha, Rituraj and many other actors, directors and Manoj's friends. Many thanks to them.

Thanks to Sharib Hashmi, who many now know as Talpade of the series *The Family Man*. Sharib shared many of his memories related to Manoj with me, and connected me with Ashok Purang, who was a major influence during the early days of Manoj's life and career. I share a special connect with Ashokji today. Through him, I was able to reach out to Barry John, Manoj's guru. Much gratitude to him.

Thanks to Amrit Sagar, who directed the film *1971*. He not only shared his memories with me but also helped me arrange pictures and connect with other people.

Truth be told, it is impossible to count the number of people who have helped shape this book and thank them individually. For all the names I am leaving out, a heartfelt thank you, because I know how your inputs have enriched this book.

I would also like to thank Garima Budhani, a fellow journalist who helped me a lot while researching for the book. She transcribed many interviews and ensured they were well-recorded. Thanks to my journalist-friend Meenakshi Kandwal, Vishnu Upadhyaya and S. Rajeev, who continually gave their valuable inputs on different chapters, helped me get in touch with people or facilitated arranging a picture.

Many thanks to the commissioning editor of Penguin Random House India Sushant Jha and editor in chief (language publishing) Vaishali Mathur. I had worked with Sushant during my stint at Aaj Tak. When I narrated the idea to Sushant, he immediately asked me to send across a mail detailing it. Vaishali's enthusiastic reply to it within ten minutes of sending the mail assured me the book would indeed see the light of day.

It is impossible to thank your parents. Their blessings are your foremost strength. And for this, I thank Prakash Mohan Pandey, Rekha Pandey, Om Prakash Paliwal and Asha Paliwal. Thanking younger brothers Prateek Pandey, Puneet Pandey and niece Ira Puranik is of no use, since it is my right to ask them for anything. But for the record, thank you.

My wife, Gauri, has tirelessly and consistently accompanied me, both in life and in my writing journey. A simple thank you would dwarf in comparison to her boundless support and devotion. She was the first person I narrated the idea for this book to. Her suggestions have helped make the book better.

As for Palash and Pihu, my kids, they are happy that their father has accomplished something meaningful, and that the book will be available in both Hindi and English. I was never fond of clicking pictures with celebrities, and coincidentally, never had one with Manoj Bajpayee, despite knowing him for nearly fifteen years.

But now that Pihu wants to get a picture clicked with him, I will try to do it at the earliest. The good part is, both kids are now old enough to read this book.

At the end, thank you to the readers, who've taken this book, or taken out the time to read it.

Endnotes

1 'Krishna Pratap Singh ka Blog: Raebareli Mein Huwa Tha Dusra Jallianwala Bagh Kand', *Lokmat Hindi*, 7 January 2020, https://www.lokmatnews.in/blog/india/second-jallianwala-bagh-scandal-took-place-in-1921-raebareli-munshiganj-genocide/

2 A weighing scale used for measuring the load of trucks and dumpers, etc.

3 Dr Rajendra Prasad, *Champaran Mein Mahatma Gandhi* (Prabhat Prakashan; 2017 edition, 2018).

4 Dr Rajendra Prasad, *Champaran Mein Mahatma Gandhi* (Prabhat Prakashan; 2017 edition, 2018).

5 http://manojbajpayee-en.itzmyblog.com/

6 'Dilip Kumar, Manoj Bajpai could work together', *Times of India*, 11 April 2003, https://timesofindia.indiatimes.com/entertainment/hindi/bollywood/news/dilip-kumar-manoj-bajpai-could-work-together/articleshow/43100987.cms (accessed 18 November 2023).

7 Rajiv M. Vijayakar, *Dharmendra: A Biography: Not Just a He-Man* (New Delhi: Rupa Publications, 2018), p. 14.

8 'Television se sukun nahi aaya hain', BBC Hindi.com, 12 April 2004, https://www.bbc.com/hindi/entertainment/story/2004/04/040412_manoj_column9

9 Manoj Bajpai, 'Belwa Diary', *Outlook*, 17 February 2017, https://www.outlookindia.com/magazine/story/belwa-diary/298474

10 'Manoj Bajpayee Exclusive Interview: Sudhir Chaudhary', YouTube, https://www.youtube.com/watch?v=VxBlKlpSjEw

11 http://manojbajpayee-en.itzmyblog.com/

12 'Sirf Ek Bandaa Kaafi Hai - Manoj Bajpayee | The Slow Interview with Neelesh Misra', YouTube, https://www. youtube.com/watch?v=qOvdla2jLpo

13 Arvind Mohan, *Mr. M.K. Gandhi ki Champaran Diary* (Prabhat Prakashan; First Edition, 2017).

14 'Guftagoo with Manoj Bajpai', YouTube, https://www. youtube.com/watch?v=S2PYOGNnEFg&t=1417s

15 Harivansh Rai Bachchan, *Basere se Door* (Rajpal Publishing; 2015 edition, 1997).

16 He was head of Goraknath peeth and known for his role in the Ram Mandir movement. He was also a Member of Parliament.

17 'The Satya about Manoj Bajpai', *Times of India*, 12 October 2002, https://timesofindia.indiatimes.com/delhi-times/the-satya-about-manoj-bajpai/articleshow/24991387.cms?from=mdr

18 'Mera Pehla Shikshak: Shamsul Islam', BBC Hindi.com, 9 March 2004, https://www.bbc.com/hindi/entertainment/ story/2004/03/040309_manoj_column5

19 'Mera Pehla Shikshak', BBC Hindi.com, 9 March 2004, https:// www.bbc.com/hindi/entertainment/story/2004/03/040309_ manoj_column5

20 Guerilla plays are spontaneous, surprise performances held in unlikely public spaces to an unsuspecting audience. During the Emergency, these were targeted against the government.

21 'Guftagoo with Manoj Bajpai', YouTube, https://www. youtube.com/watch?v=S2PYOGNnEFg&t=1413s

22 'Dilli ke Din aur Bandit Queen ka Milna', BBC Hindi.com, 23 February 2004, https://www.bbc.com/hindi/entertainment/ story/2004/02/040223_manoj_column3

23 '"Disgusting and revolting and obscene": "Bandit Queen" and the censors https://lifestyle.livemint.com/news/talking-point/

disgusting-and-revolting-and-obscene-bandit-queen-and-
the-censors-111645265552198.html#:~:text=Bandit%20
Queen%20premiered%20at%20the,would%20change%20
Indian%20cinema%20forever.

24 'Manoj Bajpayee reveals the shocking reason for hating Anubhav
    Sinha', https://www.republicworld.com/entertainment-news/
    bollywood-news/manoj-bajpayee-reveals-the-shockingreason-
    for-hating-anubhav-sinha.html

25 https://www.youtube.com/watch?v=_nAv2ACByHk&t=3608s

26 'Taqlifo aur Pareshaniyo se Mile Sansar', BBC Hindi.com,
    1 March 2004, https://www.bbc.com/hindi/entertainment/
    story/2004/03/040301_manoj_column4

27 Sankhayan Ghosh, '"We Didn't Make the Film, It Made itself":
    Ram Gopal Varma on 20 Years of Satya', Film Companion, 3
    July 2019, https://www.filmcompanion.in/features/bollywood-
    features/we-didnt-make-the-film-it-made-itself-ram-gopal-
    varma-on-20-years-of-satya/

28 'Satya: Whose truth is it anyway?' The World of Apu, 27
    April 2013, http://urbanturban21.blogspot.com/2013/04/
    satya-whose-truth-is-it-anyway.html

29 'RGV talks about the making of Satya', YouTube, The BFan,
    28 May 2013, https://www.youtube.com/watch?v=xDgVg
    SODfl8&t=741s,

30 Somya Lakhani, 'Unbelievably believable', Indian Express, 18
    July 2010, https://indianexpress.com/article/news-archive/
    web/unbelievably-believable/lite/,

31 'Sang-Sang: Manoj Bajpayee-Shabana Raza Bajpayee',
    Chavanni Chap, 8 November 2011, http://www.chavannichap.
    com/ 2011/11/blog-post_08.html

32 Anupama Chopra, 'Film review: "Kaun", starring Urmila
    Matondkar, Manoj Bajpai', India Today, 8 March 1999,
    https://www.indiatoday.in/magazine/society-and-the-arts/films/
    story/19990308-film-review-ram-gopal-varma-kaun-starring-
    urmila-matondkar-manoj-bajpai-780336-1999-03-07

33 Raveena Tandon interview by Shairoze (Dhanak TV USA), YouTube, https://www.youtube.com/watch?v=TTeUOhtGCdQ
34 https://www.facebook.com/watch/?v=593982524535992
35 'Dil Pe Mat Le Yaar! (2000)--Not So Funny' Hansal Mehta, 25 August 2011, https://hansalmehta.com/2011/08/25/dil-pe-mat-le-yaar-2000-notso-funny/.
36 'Dil Pe Mat Le Yaar! (2000)--Not So Funny' Hansal Mehta, 25 August 2011, https://hansalmehta.com/2011/08/25/dil-pe-mat-le-yaar-2000-notso-funny/
37 Khalid Mohamed, 'Manoj Bajpai has his glory day', *Khaleej Times*, 14 February 2016, https://www.khaleejtimes.com/wknd/manoj-bajpai-has-his-glory-day
38 Khalid Mohamed, 'Manoj Bajpai has his glory day', *Khaleej Times*, 14 February 2016, https://www.khaleejtimes.com/wknd/manoj-bajpai-has-his-glory-day
39 'Rekhaji Mujhe Batati thi ki Mahila ka Hath Kaise Pakre: Manoj Bajpayee', *Navbharat Times*, 20 January 2019, https://navbharattimes.indiatimes.com/entertainment/news-from-bollywood/rekha-used-to-teach-etiquettes-of-how-to-hold-a-hand-of-a-lady-says-manoj-bajpayee/articleshow/67608761.cms
40 Sukanya Verma, 'So, does Vivek live up to the hype?' Rediff. com, 27 September 2002, https://www.rediff.com/movies/2002/sep/27road.htm
41 'Manoj Bajpayee on the method to his madness', YouTube, BBC Asian Network, 24 June 2018, https://www.youtube.com/watch?v=8KR82gSF6qA
42 'Manoj Bajpayee ko Mila Hollywood Offer, Bataya Jyotishi ki Bhavishyavani Sach Hone ka Qissa', *Hindustan*, 2 August 2021, https://www.livehindustan.com/entertainment/story-manoj-bajpayeewas-offered-hollywood-film-but-astrologer-predicted-its-future-andit-turn-out-to-be-true-4284298.html

43 Jitesh Pillai, 'Veer Zara', Times of India, 15 November 2004, https:/ /m.timesofindia.com/bollywood/veer-zaara/ articleshow/923432.cms

44 Jaya Dwivedie, 'Aap ki Adalat: Disco mein nahi mila entry, phir Manoj Bajpayee ke liye Shah Rukh Khan ne kiya jugaad', India TV.in, 20 May 2023, https://www.indiatv.in/entertainment/ bollywood/manoj-bajpayee-told-in-aapki-adalat-shah-rukh- khan-borrowed-shoes-for-him-2023-05-20-962479

45 'Manoj Bajpayee talks to Atika Farooqui on childhood youth & career | Part (3/3)', YouTube, https://www.youtube.com/ watch?v=mULnU4HBGXk

46 'I was forced to change my name', 5 August 2008, Rediff. com, https://www.rediff.com/movies/2008/aug/05raza.htm

47 http://manojbajpayee-en.itzmyblog.com/

48 'ETC Bollywood Business | Tevar Opening Weekend Collection + Manoj Bajpai | Komal Nahta', YouTube, https:// www.youtube.com/watch?v=nIG9DEYhphg

49 RGV - Ram Gopal Varma Blog #31, 'Stars and Actors', http://rgv-ram-gopal-varma. blogspot.com/2013/11/ram- gopal-varma-blog-31-stars-and-actors.html

50 'Ram Gopal Varma and me', Manoj Bajpayee, 11 September 2008, http://manojbajpayee-en.itzmyblog.com/2008/09/ ram-gopal-verma-and-me.html

51 RGV - Ram Gopal Varma Blog #201 "Disrespectful Respect', http://rgv-ram-gopal-varma. blogspot.com/2013/12/ram-gopal- varma-blog-201-disrespectful.html

52 '"Ram Gopal Varma and I have patched-up": Manoj Bajpayee', NDTV, 21 January 2013, https://movies.ndtv. com/bollywood/ram-gopal-varma-and-i-havepatched-up- manoj-bajpayee-631274

53 'Ram Gopal Varma praises Manoj Bajpayee for his short film "Ouch"', Mid-Day, 2 November 2016, https://www.

mid-day.com/entertainment/bollywood-news/article/Ram-Gopal-Varma-Manoj-Bajpayee-short-film-Ouch-praises-Bollywood-News-17728184

54 Interview with Saurabh Dwivedi, 'Manoj Baypayee Bataa Rahein Hain Bure Daur Mein Kis Kis Director ko Phone Karke Kaam Maanga: Anurag Kashyap'. The Lallantop, 6 September 2018, https://www.youtube.com/watch?v=jQY7RS4a5lM

55 ibid.

56 http://manojbajpayee-en.itzmyblog.com/

57 'Need blessings for my daughter', Manoj Bajpayee, 14 March 2011, http://manojbajpayee-en.itzmyblog.com/2011/03/need-blessings-for-my-daughter.html

58 Deborah Young, 'Gangs of Wasseypur: Cannes Review', *Hollywood Reporter*, 23 May 2013, https://www.hollywood reporter.com/news/general-news/gangs-wasseypur-cannes-review-328768/

59 Subhra Gupta, 'Gangs of Wasseypur Part 1', *Indian Express*, 22 June 2012, https://indianexpress.com/article/entertainment/entertainment-others/gangs-of-wasseypur-part-i/ (now defunct)

60 Anupama Chopra, 'Anupama Chopra's review: Gangs of Wasseypur', *Hindustan Times*, 23 June 2012, https://www.hindustantimes.com/movie-reviews/anupama-chopra-sreview-gangs-of-wasseypur/story-iGAekBzJAuamgXRfcODzbJ.html

61 'Movie review: Chakravyuh', *India Today*, 2 November 2012, https://www.indiatoday.in/movies/reviews/story/bollywood-movie-review-chakravyuh-119756-2012-10-27

62 Subhra Gupta, 'Tevar short movie review', *Financial Express*, 17 January 2015, https://www.financialexpress.com/life/entertainment-tevar-short-movie-review-31016/

63 Roshmila Bhattacharya, 'Manoj Bajpayee takes us through the prep of some of his most brilliant performances', *Mumbai Mirror*, 12 May 2017, https://mumbaimirror.indiatimes.com/entertainment/bollywood/manoj-bajpayee-takes-us-through-the-prep-of-some-of-his-most-brilliant-performances/articleshow/58636981.cms

64 'Rajkummar Rao: Aligarh Not Out-of-the-Box Story', NDTV, 22 April 2015, https://www.ndtv.com/entertainment/rajkummar-rao-aligarh-not-out-of-the-box-story-757281

65 Sweta Kaushal, 'Aligarh review: Manoj Bajpayee touches your heart, changes perceptions', *Hindustan Times*, 26 February 2016, https://www.hindustantimes.com/movie-reviews/aligarh-reviewa-subtle-strong-film-on-human-rights-and-democracy/story-onV213G1c1Iky2Y8xVeG9J.html

66 Rohit Vats, 'Budhia Singh – Born To Run review: It's sleek, fast and pointed', *Hindustan Times*, 5 August 2016, https://www.hindustantimes.com/movie-reviews/budhia-singh-born-to-run-review-sleek-fast-and-pointed/story-ZuvuQZ8J8faq8x4a6rsAXJ.html

67 'Manoj Bajpayee and John Abraham reveal interesting details about Satyameva Jayate', YouTube, https://www.youtube.com/watch?v=3JlikHhNQLI